2-23-66

Give Us This Day

Give Us This Day

The Story of Sister Dulce,
the Angel of Bahia

by

NATHAN A. HAVERSTOCK

APPLETON-CENTURY

New York

First edition

APPLETON-CENTURY
AFFILIATE OF
MEREDITH PRESS

Library of Congress Catalog Card Number: 65-25359

MANUFACTURED IN THE UNITED STATES OF AMERICA FOR MEREDITH PRESS

VAN REES PRESS   •   NEW YORK

1347348

Contents

Give Us This Day

Prologue

Sнᴇ dislikes waiting. That's why she was impatient for the men to finish loading the three boxes of fish into the dilapidated trunk of the old taxi. She fretted, shifting her spare frame from one foot to the other, until the scrawny, unshaven driver who had delivered her to the ice plant screeched the rusty lid of the trunk into place, swiveled on his peg leg, and said, "Let's go, Sister."

Few would believe, looking at this Brazilian nun, weighing scarcely eighty-five pounds, that she could have accomplished so much. In less than thirty years, *Irmã* Dulce ("Sister Sweet" in English) has single-handedly established a labor union, a hospital, a refuge for the homeless, and a farm for the rehabilitation of delinquent boys. She herself would deny, of course, the reference to single-handedness, saying, "No, it's God's work," the same as the taxi driver said *"Deus é grande* [God is big-hearted]," as his cab narrowly missed a fat man crossing the street.

This is the story of Sister Dulce's charm, skill, daring, shrewdness, talent and dedication—qualities summed up by the Portuguese word *jeito* for which English has no equivalent. For years her *jeito* has represented hope to the poor of her native city of Bahia, who live in one of the most infernal spots on earth.

The slums of Bahia are called the *alagados,* wobbly houses

3

on a crescent of land reclaimed from the sea by dumping garbage into the stagnant waters of the bay of Itapagipe. The refuse provides the fill needed to extend flimsy points of land out over the water.

Before the refuse has fully decomposed, a process that occurs quickly in the tropics, the homeless rush in like squatters, to stake out their claims. To make their shacks, they scavenge anything they can legally or illegally lay their hands on: sticks, crate boxes, bits of driftwood. Desperately in need of shelter, they weave these discarded materials into a loose frame resembling wickerwork. Then, kneeling in the garbage, the homeless face each other on either side of the wickerwork frame. As they slap mud on the frame, little by little a wall emerges, which the fierce sun will bake dry.

Once four walls have been completed, the shacks are roofed over with flattened tin cans and bits of clay tile. The finished dwellings have few windows for ventilation or light, only a doorway hung with a swatch of burlap. The shacks face each other in long, precariously leaning rows across a stinking spread of refuse, punctuated by mounds where garbage trucks distributed their loads unevenly.

Barefoot children dig industriously in each fresh load of garbage, hoping to find something edible. Swarms of flies hum everywhere; black vultures, called *urubus*, keep a sharp watch for any morsels the children might have missed.

The backs of the makeshift dwellings squat over the water, supported by spindly poles which rest in the ooze of the slick bottom. Before the poles rot out, the backs like the fronts of the shacks will be supported by the accumulation of refuse. In the meantime the water is deep enough for an occasional baby to drown, and near enough the shacks to provide a dumping place for human excrements, which collects in stagnant rivulets between the fingers of higher ground.

Here in the alagados misery is a way of life. The news of

death is customarily accepted with a gentle shrug of the shoulders, a reiteration of the Brazilian cliché, "*Se Deus quiser* [If God so wills it]," and not infrequently by a docile smile like that of a humble servant in the presence of a benevolent master.

Sister Dulce is seldom far from the alagados. That's why she was so anxious for the taxi to return to her slum hospital. She was worried about the sick who were for the moment a few blocks from the care of her loving hands. She wondered whether there would be enough fish to go around. She worried about tomorrow's needs.

CHAPTER

1

Begging

THREE boys, their heads bobbing like corks on rapid water, follow a nun hurrying through the business district of Bahia, Brazil. Their shoes, sturdy sandals whose broad leather straps have worn smooth the tough, dark skin on the crowns of their feet, smack abrasively against the tiled sidewalk.

When the nun reaches the Bank of Bahia, she pauses so the boys can catch up with her. Her light blue habit and her black veil lined with shining white stand out in the pale morning sunlight. As she stops and crooks her right hand against her hip, the silver medallion of the Virgin Mary swings free from her neck, like a pendulum, across her cream-colored breastplate.

She takes the boys by the hand. Together they rush up the steep winding stairs and into the second-floor office of the bank's disbursing officer. There she turns and admonishes the boys to wait quietly.

The boys jump up into large, overstuffed chairs. In these thrones they lose themselves in the mysteries of big-format magazines, *Manchete, O Cruzeiro,* and *Fatos e Fotos.* They riffle through the pages looking for sex and scenes of violence, particularly war pictures. One holds up a cheesecake shot of a breasty woman to delight the others. The words in the magazines are wasted on them, for none of the boys, aged eleven, twelve, and fourteen, can read.

While they enjoy the pictures and the other fascinations of the bank that momentarily engage their interest—functionaries buzzing about like bees in a hive; a teller counting his way through a mountain of dirty *cruzeiro* bills—their friend, the nun, inquires into the state of her finances. She learns today, as she did yesterday and the day before, that the bank account is precariously low, inadequate to the day's necessities.

Today, for example, there is food to be bought for the sick in her hospital, wooden handles for the broom factory at her farm, and gasoline for the old green truck that carried her and the boys to the center of town, sputtering over the holes in the pavement and jostling its human cargo unmercifully. "Today," she says to the bank official, "I will have to scrape up seventy thousand cruzeiros"—equal to approximately forty dollars.

He shakes his head sympathetically. She thanks him, though he has confirmed her expectations. Each day he makes time, between signing checks and administering bank disbursements, to keep an eye on her account, which he maintains under the blotter on his desk. He advises her, too, like a family physician, on important secondary matters like exchange rates, making sure that Sister Dulce gets the most out of every penny that comes her way.

The boys make a neat stack of the magazines. They pursue the nun out into the chaotic streets. She appears not to know precisely where she is going. Suddenly, she ducks into a shop whose ornate front overhangs the sidewalk.

The shop's proprietor, a tall, lean man, sees her coming. He takes a hitch in his belt, lights a filter cigarette, and prepares to greet her warmly. He invites her into his backroom office, from which he can maintain a vigilant watch for customers through a glass partition. They have scarcely sat down before the nun breaks into a vigorous narrative.

"You know," the Sister says, "the boob who was filling the gas tank on our Volkswagen bus the other night tipped over the candle he was using to light his way to the tank and set the whole thing on fire. Pss-shoom! It all went up in flames. Fortunately, no one was hurt, but the bus is a total loss. The mechanic—you know, the one who can fix anything—happened to be nearby. He said he'll give me fifty thousand cruzeiros [$34] for what's left. Do you think he can get anything out of a completely demolished bus?"

"Well, maybe he can salvage the motor or enough spare parts to make it worth his while, but from what you say, I'd say you did well to get the fifty *contos.*"

Their conversation rambles from topic to topic. It is all engaging, agreeable talk. But, between the nun and the shopkeeper there is an unspoken thought. Each is aware that the point to the conversation is money—the money Sister Dulce must raise to feed the hundreds of people who are counting on her to feed them today as she always has in the past.

Money is tight. Inflation has outpaced all efforts to cope with it. In the last year of the Goulart regime, when Brazil was perilously close to Communism, inflation raised the cost of living by 80, some say by 100, per cent.

At last there is a long pause. She has experienced the same pause thousands of times before. In such moments she has lost friends, like the businessman who has avoided her scrupulously ever since she broke down and wept profusely when he refused her outstretched hand. Little did she realize the embarrassment of the moment for her friend. His mistress had fallen prey to venereal disease and he had been forced to acknowledge her openly to his wife. He had just come from confessing his extramarital affair to his wife.

When Sister Dulce approached him, fresh from the consequences of his tragic revelation, it had been the last straw. From that moment he seemed driven to avoid the daylight. He took a night job, watching the wharves where he might avoid the sight of Sister Dulce, while she, they say in agony because of the anguish she had chanced to cause her friend, prayed for his soul and sheltered his mistress until the dark young girl died suddenly at the height of a burning fever.

Sister Dulce has never become accustomed to the sensations of this moment when she must persist in seeking alms. Perhaps she feels uneasy because she was brought up in a family that didn't need to beg. She looks so tense at these times that one might expect her to break out crying at the slightest untoward sound or gesture. Her enemies accuse her of using the prospect of a scene as a weapon in her arsenal of feminine wiles. But she herself says candidly, "This begging all the time is hard work. It's frustrating. It gets progressively worse as I get further and further into debt."

She squirms a little in her chair while she waits. She coughs nervously. Finally she realizes by the length of the silence, by the way her friend turns away his eyes, that today it's hopeless. He can't give her any money.

She withdraws graciously. She thanks him for all his past kindnesses. Undeterred by disappointment, she makes her way out onto the street again, where the boys have been waiting and weighing among themselves the chances for something to eat. At the corner the Sister stops before a fruit stand. She buys each of them an apple.

She asks one of the boys to hand her the little brown zipper case where she keeps her bills. While the boys devour the apples, everything but the stems, she rustles through a handful of bills and mutters to herself, "Seventy thousand cruzeiros." Off they go.

The Sister hurries along and into a corner office building

named after its owner, Manoel Joaquim de Carvalho. Inside
the boys settle down on a long, stiff bench in a stony, cold
waiting room whose walls reach up two stories. The Sister
threads her way through a maze of desks, past junior execu-
tives and secretaries, to the office of the owner of a huge
import-export business, none other than Manoel Joaquim
himself.

The confident, graying business baron looks up from his
work, smiling indulgently at her audacious entrance. Facing
him, at the other side of two heavily polished desks, sits his
fat-faced son. The younger Manoel, attired in a white suit
cut from the same bolt of Irish linen as his father's, looks up
too and smiles kittenishly.

The younger Manoel is totally absorbed with his extra-
curricular interest in philosophy. His work *L'Essence d'être*
(The Essence of Being), has recently been published in
France. At a tremendous cost in time and effort he has collected all the reviews of it, from a short paragraph clipped
from a Bahian daily paper to a sentence or two in some ob-
scure Belgian journal. He has had all these reviews retyped
and duplicated. He presses a set of the reviews on visitors,
explaining that now he is hoping to have his work published
in English. "Do you know of any press that might be interested?"

Sister Dulce scarcely seems to see him at all; she ignores
his smile. She bends toward the elder Manoel. She asks him
for the gold book that he keeps in his top right-hand drawer.
Over the years he has helped her to fill the book with the
names of one hundred and fifty Bahian business firms that
can be counted on to contribute regularly to her work. On
each page there is the rubber-stamped seal of a firm and a
specified sum of money pledged to Sister Dulce. But now
the pledges have been devalued by inflation. The money that

comes in regularly is a drop in the bucket compared to her needs.

While her graceful fingers race through the pages, she and the elder Manoel discuss likely people to visit for the money she needs today. He speaks with polite interest, mentioning acquaintances who have turned a good profit lately, but his mind is preoccupied elsewhere.

They commiserate over the inflation that makes money worthless overnight. Under the strain of fruitless small talk, the Sister becomes increasingly agitated. Her face looks drawn and pale. Her spare frame shakes violently from dry coughing, the chronic bronchitis that follows her everywhere.

She takes her leave abruptly. The fresh air outside and the commotion of the street seem to revive her. She looks like a boat that has been pushed off the sand into the water. Under full sail, a light breeze billowing out her habit, she tacks toward a building a block away. The building superintendent, who sits behind the desk in the lobby, greets her with deference. Yes, the man she hopes to see is in.

The icy air conditioning in the executive's large, well-appointed office rejuvenates the boys, who are tired from traipsing around the city. Goose pimples stand out on their brown skins.

A handsome businessman, looking curiously tweedy for the tropics, rises from behind his desk. With his left hand on the switch of an intercom he calls for an assistant. The Sister sits gingerly on the edge of her chair.

"Get me a draft for fifty thousand cruzeiros, payable to Sister Dulce," the executive tells his assistant.

A warm smile suffuses the face of the nun. She relaxes back into the chair, and launches happily into a retelling of the day's gossip: the burning of the Volkswagen, the progress at the farm, the spiraling inflation—the problems of her network of activities in which the businessman takes a keen, professional interest.

He offers to show her the plans he has had drawn for the construction of a new textile factory. She comments on them intelligently. As she does so, she is reminded of a past kindness. She tells him how much she appreciates the sheets that he supplied for her entire hospital. "They are good sheets. They hold up well," she tells him. He is obviously pleased by her compliments.

She wants to show him exactly how his fifty thousand cruzeiros will be spent. Her beautiful hand gropes around in the brown zipper bag, searching out the monthly list of expenses which Adalicio, her volunteer bookkeeper, prepared for her. But she doesn't find it, even though she walks her slender fingers back and forth through all the papers five or six times. All the while, she talks and listens. Finally, she gives up. "I guess I don't have it. Well, no matter, you can imagine how the cost of electricity, gasoline, and all the other things we need has gone up in recent times."

The businessman nods understandingly. He bends over to sign the draft that has been slipped on the desk in front of him. After some more talk, more details passed back and forth on one another's enterprises, the Sister rises to go. "Remember me to your daughter. She must be a big girl now. Do you remember how she came to help me when she was only three years old? She brought flowers for the patients nearly every day, it seems. And she gave me her beautiful birthday doll. We raffled it off and made a lot of money. Just think, only three years old and such a little saint!"

For several more hours, somewhere in this vast city of 700,000 people, the Sister and the boys continue the search for twenty thousand more cruzeiros. The search is an interesting one, taking Sister Dulce and the boys into the offices of government officials, a variety of stores, and the shops of artisans. Along the way they pick up donations for Sister Dulce's work, ranging from a box of cigars to a stringless guitar.

The search ends at twilight, as the fishermen out in the bay are hauling in the nets cast out with care in the predawn hours. Here and there in the business district, squeezed between the bay and the sharp hills, storekeepers close their shops. There is an upsurge of pedestrian traffic toward the elevator and the cog-railed inclines that carry people from the business district in the lower city to their homes on the high promontory.

The statue of Castro Alves, the poet of the slaves, overlooks the rush of traffic and the sea below. The title of his poem, "Whoever Gives to the Poor Makes a Loan to God," seems appropriate to the nun's mission.

The Sister and the boys return footsore to the green truck whose driver has been patiently waiting all day. He smiles at them, sensing that once again the Sister has filled the daily need.

Tomorrow the driver will have to give up his job. His last X-ray shows that he again has tuberculosis. He must go back into the hospital for some bed rest. The Sister must figure out how to replace him. This will be a tough job; good drivers are hard to come by. She searches her thoughts for an answer to this new problem on the way back to the Albergue Santo Antônio, the hospital built by her determination to serve Bahia's slums.

The truck moves slowly on the single main artery out of the lower city. It comes to a halt in front of the military base where several Go-Slow signs stand in the middle of the narrow street. Each sign is guarded by a boy-faced soldier with a tommygun slung carelessly over his shoulder.

Bored faces, arranged like those on the photograph of a high-school graduating class, peer out from over the base's heavy wrought-iron gate. As the truck passes, two or three of them flash smiles of recognition at the Sister.

Next the truck passes the railroad station where families wait for a ride south, to some place out of the hungry Brazilian Northeast, some place where a man can hope to find a job to support his family.

The truck stops in back of the Albergue. There, in a small courtyard, a throng of people—old women, young mothers with frail sick babies wrapped in dirty shawls, homeless boys —wait to have a word with Sister Dulce. She is tired and presses her thumb against the center of her forehead to numb the pain of a headache.

She listens to each one. They are all hungry so she sends someone across the street for some freshly baked bread from her Refuge, a free hostel for poor transients. The sack of bread circulates. It disappears as if bewitched.

A toothless hag works her way to the Sister. "Remember me, Sister Dulce," she says. "You said I could always count on receiving a cup of milk." Sister Dulce sends her into the kitchen.

A skinny woman marches past, pressing a cloth pad against her cheek as if she had a toothache. At a short distance from the knot of petitioners, she stops and breaks into a weird grin that turns into a cackling, uncontrolled laugh. She babbles a torrent of profanities.

No one takes any notice of her. Everyone has forgotten when or why it was that she went mad. But no one bothers her. Around and around the hospital she goes, always with the wad of cloth jammed up against her cheek.

The Sister sees everyone. Some want medicine. Others want permission to spend the night across the street at the Refuge. A young woman holds out a grubby baby girl whom she says she found on the train tracks down by the railroad station. She wants the Sister to keep the baby.

Sister Dulce says, "Yes, my child," and she takes the baby tenderly in her arms. The nun knows the woman is lying, that the baby is her own, and that she wants to be rid of it, perhaps because the new man she is living with doesn't want it.

Maybe that's he, standing sheepishly on down the street, taking in the proceedings out of the corner of his eye. Whatever the reason, it makes no difference. Sister Dulce accepts the baby willingly. She knows that the woman will no longer care for it.

Over against the wall there is another woman, whose child died in the hospital that morning. Sister Dulce, still cradling the baby she just received, goes over to comfort her. "It's better, don't you see? It's better that your little one died. Otherwise he would have been an impossible burden to you. You already have so many children. Take care of them. Get over this sadness. You have a great deal to do. Your other children need you."

The woman dries her eyes. A little later, her face flushed with grief, she walks off quietly to her home in the slums nearby.

Suddenly the Sister breaks away from the center of the pulsating little group of people that surrounds her whenever she stops. She hears something: a frail boy weeping. She recognizes him. "Why are you crying, my son? Why did you leave the farm?"

"Because he beat me. The master beat me for no reason." The child refers to an older boy who has the responsibility for the discipline of some of the young boys at Sister Dulce's farm. She can see that the older boy has beaten him severely. His hands are raw from the blows of the paddle.

She comforts him. She tells him that he can eat dinner at the hospital and spend the night. "But tomorrow I will take you out to the farm again. Believe me, my son, it is better for you there. You'll see. There is more to do. What could you accomplish by staying here? No, my son, you must go back to the farm." The boy isn't happy with the decision, but he resigns himself to it. The thought of an Albergue meal cheers him. So, too, do the warm, wise words of the Sister, whose picture he carries in the single celluloid card holder of his frayed wallet.

Once all her petitioners have been taken care of, the Sister goes inside the Albergue to her plain office, where she puts the brown zipper bag into the desk drawer on top of her well-read copy of *The Little Prince*. From across the hall she hears the monotonous noise of evening prayers. She has missed them again. By now the Sister Superior is accustomed, if not reconciled, to her frequent absences.

The noise of dinner preparations in the hospital wards is agreeable to Sister Dulce's ears. She has gotten through another day. She presses her thumb to her forehead again. As she does so, into her office slips a small, freckle-faced, red-headed boy with an ingratiating smile.

She hasn't seen him before. "Yes," she tells him, "you are welcome to eat with us tonight, but tomorrow you must go to the farm." The boy, perhaps the issue of a sailor's pleasure, does a happy little jig.

The Sister reminds him that he can't have dinner until he takes a shower and washes himself thoroughly with a bar of strong soap. The redhead grins. While the Sister leans forward over her desk, staring into its veneered surface as if looking for the answer to a perplexing problem, the redhead takes off all his clothes and throws them in a heap on the floor.

Stark naked, he hoots fiendishly at the astonished look that dawns on her weary face. The Sister chides him, "You can't take off your clothes in here, my son." But before she can repair the damage, the boy bounds out of her office and down the hall, past the kitchen, and into the shower.

2

Bahia

Sɪsᴛᴇʀ Dulce's native city of Salvador, commonly called Bahia, was officially founded in 1548. Situated on the spacious and beautiful Bay of All Saints, Bahia has a good natural harbor, located centrally on the Brazilian coastline. From the city's commanding heights, the Portuguese reasoned that Bahia could be protected from the raids of marauding corsairs.

Bahia has a special, even unique, character—partly African, stemming from the extensive use of slave labor to work the sugar-cane plantations, partly Dutch, dating from the brief Dutch occupation of the city in the seventeenth century, but mostly Portuguese, dating from the two centuries when Bahia was the capital of Portugal's New World empire of Brazil.

During this period, the Portuguese were lavish in adorning Bahia. The popular notion that Bahia has a church for every day of the year, while an exaggeration, has its origins in the Portuguese determination to decorate Bahia with cathedrals, like São Francisco and its dazzling golden interior, which rival those of Lisbon for grace and elegance. The recently appointed bishop of Bahia, who set aside a Sunday to visit every church in the city, discovered that he had thus committed nearly one hundred and fifty Sundays.

The afterglow of Bahia's prestige as Brazil's first city

lasted until the early nineteenth century when the Portuguese monarch, forced to flee Portugal to escape capture by the victorious legions of Napoleon, stopped in Bahia for a stay before—reluctantly, according to Bahians—relocating his court in Rio de Janeiro. After the departure of John the Sixth and his court, Bahia steadily continued to slip in importance before the growth of the cities of the South, Rio de Janeiro and São Paulo. Nonetheless, Bahia is a proud city which has carefully nurtured the traditions of aristocracy. In recent years Bahia has spent itself recklessly in constructing a modern theatre, restoring a colonial church as a Museum of Sacred Art, and sponsoring gatherings of the learned.

Within the Luso-Brazilian civilization, that cultural heritage which Portuguese sailors diffused during the great age of exploration when they carried the Portuguese language and culture to the farflung corners of the world (for example, Macao in China, Angola in Africa and Brazil in the New World), Bahia has been a focal point for the study of Portugal's seafaring enterprise.

One of the proudest moments in recent Bahian history occurred in 1959 when the city was host to a Colloquium on Luso-Brazilian Studies, a gathering of scholars of many nationalities. Learned men, like Charles Boxer of England (better known to some as Emily Hahn's husband), whose contribution to Bahian history is documented in several books, were welcomed like conquering heroes.

At the airport a bevy of young girls who carry on, in the name of their organization, *Bandeirantes,* Brazil's frontier tradition, marched off with the luggage of each visiting scholar under their arms. The Bandeirantes, the equivalent of girl scouts, are named after the pioneer families which set out from São Paulo centuries ago to seek their fortunes in the thick forests of the Mato Grosso. Lured on by tales of gold and precious stones, some of these original Bandeirantes eventually settled the interior of the state of Bahia.

Seldom has a city so completely turned itself over to such a celebration of its past. As one of the scholars said, "I have never been the object of such adulation. Here, I am like the Messiah come again. In my university, I am just another lecturer."

The two-week orgy of scholarship began with a high Mass celebrated in the new Museum of Sacred Art. The Mass was presided over by a tall Negro priest, a native of Bahia, and by the Cardinal resplendent in his red robes. Off to the side of the altar stood a plump Dominican friar, whose hands were still wet with the painting he had been doing the night before to finish the restoration of the Museum.

From the Mass the scholars went to sample their first full-scale Bahian meal. Bahia has its own cuisine. There are dishes like *vatapá*, made of flour, shrimp, chunks of fish, peanuts and *dendê*. Dendê, an oil extracted from the African oil palm, is used in the preparation of several Bahian dishes. Besides being good for the digestion, dendê has a pleasing flavor, suggestive of Italian olive oil. During their stay, the scholars savored other dishes with sonorous names like *carurú* (pronounced kye-roo-roo), made from okra, with shrimp, fish, and chicken and seasoned with herbs, dendê, and with local peppers which have a flavor like tabasco.

Each new meal had its own setting, a coconut grove by the beach; the sparkling white tablecloths of *La Ondina*, a restaurant set on a hillside with such a commanding view of the ocean and the sky that one appears to be quite near the warm tropical moon and the Southern Cross; or the leisurely confusion of the Hotel da Bahia, whose restaurant overlooks a pleasing square and a formal garden decorated with statues.

There was something to match each scholar's interest: dazzling churches for art historians; the Africanisms which have crept into Bahian speech for linguists; native dancing and song for musicologists. An elderly academician from Europe, whose publications include several on windmills, found himself enchanted with the cleverness of Bahian fishing boats.

The only sour note was sounded by the large contingent of Portuguese from Portugal, who fell to feuding immediately upon their arrival with their New World cousins. One would have thought that since everything was free of charge, the Portuguese for once could have forgotten their ancient animosities. But no. Some of them complained about the accommodations which they had been assigned in the lovely São Francisco retreat; others about imaginary slights in the scheduling of the presentation of scholarly papers. They manifested, in short, what one of their numbers candidly summed up as: "That deep sense of inferiority which I have noticed that overly stuffy Englishmen show towards their colleagues from the United States."

But, like gentlemen, the visitors from Portugal avoided an incident. As the weeks wore on their mutterings grew softer before the impressive spectacle of Bahia. The Bahians, for their part, kept up a steady stream of propaganda to placate the visitors from Portugal, impressing upon them their deep sense of obligation to the seafaring skill of Portugal, which had brought the rich traditions of the Old World to the New.

And when the Colloquium drew to a conclusion, the scholars left Bahia quite unaware for the most part that the city has a seamy side. So pleased were they, so well fed and comfortable, that when the copilot of one airplane rushed down the aisle just as the plane was gaining altitude over the bay, looked out the window and exclaimed, "The wheels won't retract!" the whole planeful of scholars laughed. And they were still laughing after the plane had rolled to a stop again on its return to the airport at Bahia for repairs.

Even the Portuguese, who might have been expected to

see some sort of plot in this incident, were undisturbed. It is entirely possible, as the Bahians had demonstrated without any malice or conscious wish to deceive, to enjoy the city of Bahia with a kind of perfect contentment. Bahia has a fascination and a charm which cast a spell.

The spell perhaps begins in Bahia's unusual topography. The city is laid out on three levels. The lowest is a narrow strip of flatland which follows the irregular coastline for more than twenty miles. Along the Atlantic coast there is a series of distinctive beaches, more than twenty in all. There is, as Bahians point out, a beach for every taste; calm and serene beaches like Barra, and wild and dangerous beaches like Itapuan (pronounced E-top-oo-on), whose very name sounds out the crashing of a roller.

The Atlantic beaches are open and uncluttered except for an occasional hut or grove of palms in whose shade fishermen repair their nets. During the day, fishermen perch precariously on rafts, called *jangadas,* strapped onto crude wooden seats. Before dawn until long after dark, they fish off the reefs which parallel the coastline. The jangada is their home; the sea, their challenge. Overhead a curious, sand-colored sail propels the flimsy vessel to and from the fishing grounds. The triangular sail is extended to the wind by a long yardarm slung from the short mast. The fisherman navigates by experience, steering his craft with a paddle and movable lee-boards which help to stabilize the jangada in the water. The raft looks curiously Oriental, giving the impression from a distance of a small Chinese junk. Its silhouette is awkward, too low on the water for the pounding Atlantic waves which wash over the light, buoyant logs much of the time. The salt water and the sun score the fisherman's feet with deep blisters.

The sight of the fishermen and the sound of their tragic sea-chanties have strongly influenced the character of Bahia.

The misfortunes of simple fishermen, through sudden storms and bad luck, seem to sum up the struggle of Bahia, as endless and as restless as the comings and goings of fishermen who brave the perils of the deep.

Their vicissitudes have found lyric expression in the songs of Dorival Caymmí, a Brazilian singer born in Bahia in 1914, the same year as Sister Dulce. His songs, whose themes provide, incidentally, a fitting accompaniment to the life of Sister Dulce, weave a spell which aptly expresses the region —a scent of nostalgia, the sparkle of a golden tooth, pride mixed with despair, and suffering before the forces of nature like the sea.

After dark, Caymmí's songs, played fast, enliven a barefoot dance on the beach. *Cachaça,* a sugar-cane liquor, deadens the nerves so the subtle rhythm of the samba can take over. In nightclubs, called *boites,* a soft rendition of his music is played in a darkness lighted only by the penlights carried by waiters to illuminate the menus and the checks. Against this background, his music provides a perfect setting for soft conversation and hands moist from a lover's clasp.

As a boy the mulatto Caymmí sold soda pop by barking in a loud voice along the beaches of Bahia. He went often with his brother to the beach at Itapuan to swim and to drink and dance and sing in the company of fishermen. He expressed the fisherman's life in words and simple melodies which, from the standpoint of subtle poignancy, are forerunners of *bossa nova.*

Of the samba, a dance of African origin, which is a blend of dip and swing much more energetic than the tango, Caymmí sang,

> "I was born in the samba,
> The samba is in my genes,
> From the curse of the samba
> I will never be free."

Of his boyhood, he wrote the classic song, "I Don't Have Any Place to Live":

> "I don't have any place to go
> And so I live on the sand.
> I was born very little
> Like everybody else.
> But everyone else grew straight;
> I'm the only twisted one.
> That's why I live near the edge of the sea,
> Depending on what God gives me.
> My Maria lives with some other girls;
> I pay Maria's rent."

The homelessness of a boy living by the sea is a theme in Bahian literature, too, in one of the novels of Jorge Amado, which is a narrative of the tragedy of homeless boys who organize a gang in an abandoned, rat-infested warehouse by the sea.

Of all Caymmí's songs, the one which best conveys the idea of Bahia is "Longing for Bahia," a song which he popularized with his deep, resonant voice and the lilting accompaniment of his guitar. The word "longing" in the song title is the Portuguese word *"saudade,"* which, according to the dictionary, means "the sweet and sad remembrance of distant or deceased persons or places, accompanied by the desire to return, to see them again, or to possess them."

> "Ah, what a longing I have for Bahia.
> If I had only listened to my mother.
> 'You aren't going to leave your sick mother, are you?'
> If people only did what their hearts tell them to—
> But this world is full of evil and illusion.
> Ah, if I had only listened, I wouldn't be suffering so.
> I wouldn't have this longing in my breast,

This longing like a cancer.
I should at least be entitled to
Someone who could hear my confession.
Put yourself in my place,
And see how an unhappy man suffers,
Who can't unburden himself
By confessing to the whole world what no one else
    can confess for him.
See the bind I'm in,
How my poor heart suffers,
A person who believed
That glory and money could make him happy."

Caymmí's stories of fishermen unravel the simple theme of risk and death, and the forces that compel fishermen to leave their families to earn a living on the sea. According to one lament,

"It is sweet to die in the sea,
In the green waves of the sea."

In 1953 the people of Bahia named the square nearest the beach at Itapuan after Caymmí. It was a singularly appropriate honor for the singer who had expressed so beautifully not only the sadness but also the happy side of their native city. The sparkle of Bahia—gold bracelets, silk shirts and sandals—launched Caymmí's career in 1939 when his song, "What Is It That a Bahian Girl Has?" achieved instant success and recognition for the singer.

The north-south coastline turns sharply inland toward the west at the Fortress of St. Anthony, one of several strong points built in the sixteenth and seventeenth centuries to defend the city against the incursions of the Dutch, who were anxious to seize a part of northern Brazil for themselves. Then the coastal strip describes an east-west arc, and here is the so-called "lower city," the commercial and banking center, fronting on the harbor and on the romantic ruins of the round fortress of St. Marcellus, once another bastion in the city's defense and now a favorite rendezvous for lovers.

The lower city is the center for the economy of a large area. Like Recife, its arch rival to the north, Bahia serves as the middleman for the profits of plantations located along the humid, fertile coast. Sugar cane, transplanted by the Portuguese from the Azores, thrives on coastal soils, as does cotton, cocoa, and tobacco. The tobacco was the most highly prized exchange for African slaves when Bahia (until Brazil abolished slavery in 1889) was a center for the slave trade. Yankee clippers, bound for the United States, picked up their black cargoes in Bahia. In recent times, cocoa has become Bahia's most important export; the State of Bahia alone accounts for nearly a third of the world's cocoa.

The tragic inheritance of an economy based on the plantation system and on the exploitation of people to raise a few commodities has been detailed in works of great sociological and literary merit, like Gilberto Freyre's *Masters and Slaves* and the novels of Jorge Amado. The profits of the land find their way into the money belts of the rich in Bahia's lower city.

In the less luxurious sections of the lower city, artisans practice their crafts. In one of the oldest districts are the shoemakers; in another the carpenters. In still another, whores ply their ancient and on the whole respectable—by Bahian standards—profession.

A conversation with a whore can be an enlightening experience. To begin with, she can't understand why anybody would want to talk to her. She can't squelch a belly laugh when she learns that she will earn half again her normal rate for answering some questions. She is quite attractive. "I could

Maria Rita Lopes Pontes (Sister Dulce) as a schoolgirl. Shortly after this picture was taken, she asked her father's permission to become a nun. *Anthony R. Worley, Bahia, Brazil*

Medical facilities are still far from perfect, but progress is being made. Here a Brazilian volunteer doctor. José Stanchi Corrêa, right, examines an X-ray with the assistance of Dr. Jack Curns. *Anthony R. Worley, Bahia, Brazil*

As a child Sister Dulce played in this small park in front of the Church of Our Lady of Mercy, which formerly housed the convent of the Missionary Sisters of the Immaculate Conception. Beyond the wall to the left of the Church is the sea. *Anthony R. Worley, Bahia, Brazil*

Dr. Curns and Nurse Lucille Lebeau treat a small Brazilian boy for worms he picked up while walking on garbage in the *alagados*. Although conditions are improving, these minor ailments are often accompanied by much more serious medical problems. *Anthony R. Worley, Bahia, Brazil*

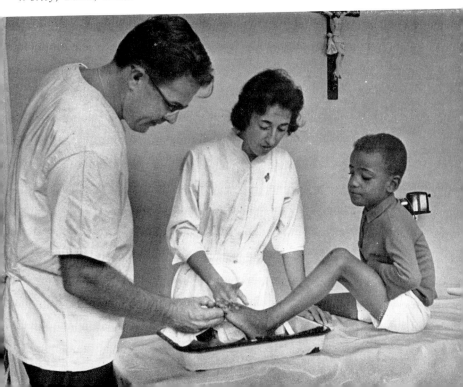

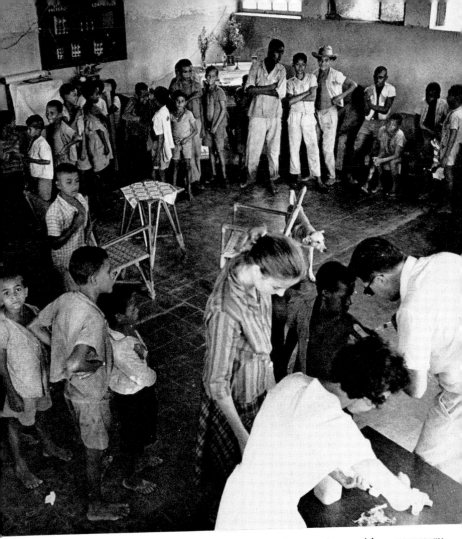

Dr. Curns and Nurse Lebeau inject reluctant boys with a necessary "triple dose." In order to gather the boys together, an announcement was made about an important meeting. Many boys, however, escaped by hiding in the tall grass outside the classroom. *Anthony R. Worley, Bahia, Brazil*

On one of her countless rounds to inspect the living conditions of her neighbors, Sister Dulce here poses with a typical Brazilian farmer of the area. *Anthony R. Worley, Bahia, Brazil*

During a routine tour of the broom factory, Sister Dulce listens carefully to a report from her foreman. *Anthony R. Worley, Bahia, Brazil*

This little boy with a bandage on his head is grateful for a short but important lesson from Sister Dulce in the joys of looking at a book. This may well become one of his few happy childhood memories. *Anthony R. Worley, Bahia, Brazil*

The famous and beautiful seaport of Salvador, the capital of Bahia, shows clearly the wide range of living conditions which still exist. The "respectable" business establishments of the upper city tower over the slums at the water's edge. Elevator at left is only direct route between the two sections of the city. *Photo from European*

A "Captain of the Sands," the Bahian term for a juvenile delinquent, is interviewed by the author. The boy, when asked his name, gave one aloud and then crudely lettered another on the pad offered to him. *Anthony R. Worley, Bahia, Brazil*

Sister Dulce and a barefoot Brazilian boy talk about his future in a quiet corner of the convent. The spiritual and material aid she can give is steadily growing, but still falls far short of the demanding needs which confront her daily. *Leonard Nadel*

earn more money, if they would only let me make arrangements in hotel lobbies. As it is, I guess I'm lucky to have run into such a good-hearted woman, the woman who runs our house."

Her story is disarmingly simple. "I come from a town you would never have heard of, in the interior of the state. I got pregnant; he came to live with me. But he could never keep a job. So there I was, waking up one day with two small children and no man to look after us. I had a cousin here in Bahia. She said, 'Why don't you come to Bahia? It would be easier to find something to do.' So I came, but something to do, that's a laugh! There's nothing for a girl without education and fine manners here."

She left her children in the care of an aunt. She ran quite casually into her present employer, a very nice woman who looks after her and several other girls who bring men off the street to their rooms. The only thought that seemed to bring a tear to her eyes was the gratitude she felt to the madam. "She is so good to us. She takes care of us when we are sick. She pays us even when we don't work sometimes. And she knows how I love my children. Every two or three months, she tucks a bus ticket for home under my pillow so I can go and visit them."

Then, suddenly, the prostitute returns to her new role. "Why don't you come with me?" She presses her taut buttock against her interviewer's hip as they sit on the hard stone bench. She feels so skeletal, so unenticing, poor thing. It is hard to fathom economic necessity of such proportions as hers, but at the same time it is easy to understand.

Further on to the west, the narrow coastal flatland ends in a peninsula. The alagados, where Sister Dulce has her hospital, are located on the leeward side of this peninsula, facing a stagnant, putrid tidal flat.

The lower city is linked with the upper city by numerous

ladeiras, narrow, treacherously steep brick or cobblestone streets, which are unscalable in a heavy rain. On a hot day there is no sound quite like the reverberation of a garbage can lid, shaken loose by a hungry cat, as it rolls down a ladeira. The upper city, where the rich live overlooking the bay, is also reached by two or three mechanical cog-wheeled trolleys, and by a cattle-sized set of elevators which jut out from the high ground of the promontory in the shape of an inverted L.

Between these two levels, there is a sporadic movement of men in three-piece white or black suits. A Bahian artist suggests that the suits, which belong to the fair-skinned descendants of the European colonizers, seems curiously disembodied. The rich to whom they belong live in a fantasy world, remote from the sensuous, freakish, rolling spectacle of Bahian life. They seldom stop in their more or less regular rounds, except at their offices or at other specific locations where they have business, or at the restaurants where they dine with predictable monotony. The rich live quite apart from the bustle of the city, like tourists on a leisurely, never-ending holiday. Their homes crown the high ground, of which there is a great deal for miles along the coastline. They live in neighborhoods, behind thick walls that hermetically seal them off from the poor. They enjoy Bahia as the beautiful postcard it is, at even the slightest distance.

Along the grand Seventh of September Avenue, named in honor of Brazilian Independence Day, some have their baronial dwellings. Each of the old and established mansions has a blue and white tile set into the wall next to the street entrance. The tile says, subtly but emphatically, "V.N."—meaning *vigia noturna* (night watchman).

Behind one of the biggest and thickest walls lives the financier Manoel Carvalho. His mansion, a huge pile of stone and masonry, is visible through openings in iron gates so ponderous and high that they might do as the Gates of Heaven.

Inside there is an oval-shaped reception hall as big as a ballroom, where visitors wait after they have been announced. Here, on one of two eight-foot settees curved to match the shape of the room and the design of the inlaid Italian-marble floor, the footsteps of the host are audible, echoing through the halls and corridors long before his arrival.

Out back, on the side of the mansion that overlooks the bay, tiers of steps drop down to a quiet, shaded terrace where a panoramic view of the bay is framed by a low, tiled wall and two enormous trees.

The feeling of the place is that of a burial vault, empty except for aristocratic ghosts and still air. There is a spiritual oppression that begins perhaps in the marble window sills and ends in the blue water, so far below that one cannot hear the noise of oars against gunwales.

Across the street there is a two-hundred-year-old manga-beira tree, so huge that municipal officials couldn't figure out any way of removing it. So there it was left to stand, completely blocking the brick sidewalk and producing its round, orange-colored fruits, which are customarily eaten when they are over-ripe, and its milky juice, a kind of latex which children shape into rubber balls to play with.

Behind the tree, a little further on down the avenue, there is a fine, old, yellow stucco house, once the great house, or master's mansion, on a plantation. The house is now a *pensão* (pension) run by a German family named Jensen. All three floors have tall rooms, some with ceilings as high as eighteen feet. The extra height keeps the house cooler by day; at night it provides a playing ground for chameleon-like lizards.

The pensão is bustling with the activities of an international crowd: a male student of the dance from Rio de Janeiro; an American technician, in Bahia to help her Harvard-professor boss find a cure for Chagas disease, at present incurable and usually fatal; a Swiss lady working for a commercial firm; and an overly glandular girl, who is like a radio station, informing everyone in a loud voice of the day's events.

"It is all quite crazy that we should be here in Brazil," says one of the white-haired Jensen ladies, "but here we are, refugees from the war. And we love it." Along with them, the Jensens brought German *Gemütlichkeit:* the spring-loaded metal clamps that hold down the hand-embroidered table cloths; the overstuffed furniture one associates with World War I movies on German themes; and dreary pictures of the Black Forest, which succeed in making the walls look terribly dark and forbidding. And yet these somber trappings only serve to heighten the hustle and bustle of the guests who speak Portuguese, German, English, French, Italian, Argentine Spanish, and other languages, and whose interests are at least as varied as their idioms.

Among the fine old and new mansions rise fashionable modern apartment buildings which provide luxurious shelter for a few. The few congregate in places like the Yacht Club, where a dainty little cable car topped by a gay striped awning delivers them from the street entrance above to a magnificent pool and promenade below. There, they dine and drink and amuse themselves at tables arranged like a flight of sea gulls hovering over the marina, where private yachts tug listlessly at their moorings.

Between the manicured homes of the rich in the upper city and the noisy commerce of the lower city, there is a third, much less distinct, level. It is formed by pockets in the terrain as it wriggles in and around, almost playfully, between the heights and the sea. Here, where a tiny middle class was beginning to emerge, Sister Dulce was born on May 26, 1914.

Fortunately, the Lopes Pontes family was always moderately well off. The father, a short, spare man with a brushlike moustache, was, and still is, a successful dentist. Industrious, capable, shrewd, he was raising his young family with devotion when tragedy struck without warning.

His wife died in childbirth in 1923. Little Maria Rita, the future Sister Dulce, became the apple of her father's eye. As the elder of two daughters in a family of six children, she assumed heavy responsibilities. She became, according to her father, a grown-up overnight. She comforted her brothers and sisters. To this day they remember her as a second mother.

Her father looks back across the years to his wife's death as if it happened only yesterday. He still wears the closely pinched high collar popular in the twenties. He talks animatedly about those promising years after the First World War when much of the world was pinning its hopes for peace on the League of Nations. He cherishes the autographed photograph given him by his fellow Bahian, Rui Barbosa, Brazil's great internationalist and delegate to The Hague. The photo shows the Brazilian champion of world order, stooped hard at work on the manuscript of a code of international law.

With her father's guidance, Maria and the other children often reenacted, with painstaking attention to authenticity of dress, the historical events which were important in shaping their country and their native city. She remembers especially well the details of the drama played each July second, on Bahia's Independence Day. There was the triumphal entry of the militia into Bahia, the show of trophies and arms taken in the bloodless struggle for independence.

A gifted natural leader, the young girl—her round head covered with rich dark bangs that ended like a knight's visor over her intent eyes—admired strength of character and action in her heroes. She twisted the historical record to heighten these qualities. She was drawn to violent themes with forceful heroines. She liked to take the role of the nun, Joana Angélica, who blocked the doorway of her convent during a time of revolution. The nun preferred the death she earned on the blade of a sword to allowing the soldiers to defile her convent's sanctity.

Soon after the death of her mother the girl in bangs began to participate in the drama of the life around her. She found that she could play a strong role, not unlike that of some of her heroines, by inviting the poor and needy into her home, of which she was the small mistress. She began by preparing meals for stray beggars and vagrants. With her father's encouragement, she invited homeless waifs to sleep overnight in a comfortable bed before returning to roam the streets.

She became fascinated with the poor. In Bahia the poor are everywhere, like litter in an artist's studio. On the street, for example, a tattered old woman stirs *acarajé*, fried patties made from a bean paste. Like one of the fates, she stirs them round and round, endlessly and methodically, in a black caldron. Proud in her tatters, she stirs as if time and the hot grease would go on bubbling forever. "Acarajé," she whines in her hollow voice whether anyone is near or not, "acarajé."

On another street a blind man picks out a droll melody on a guitar. His fingers move jerkily; his eyes stare out through dark glasses set with cheap, hazy glass. A sighted boy, perhaps the blind man's son, shakes a tambourine and carries an uncertain tune in his changing voice. The man listens above the feeble song for the clink of metal in the cup that the boy carries. The boy stares into the cup, spotted with a few filthy bronze coins.

In Bahia the poor are everywhere the public is allowed. In an alleyway a man, who shields his head from the sun with a folded newspaper hat, tries to sell to passers-by the corpses of three week-old fish. Near him, in the doorway of a vacant building, another man sits next to a mat that holds a little stack of fruit for sale. His advertisement is a papaya split open, exposing its steely blue seeds to the mildly inquisitive glance of an occasional pedestrian. A swarm of fruit flies buzzes interminably around the fruit.

There were when Sister Dulce was a girl, as there are today, endless variations. Each winding street soon loses itself in a sea of houses and shops, makeshift markets, and in different sets of people in a shifting scene.

The shops have lively signs. One bears the name of a Caymmí song, "What Is It That a Bahian Girl Has?" Others are called "Star of the Sea" and "Everything with God." Very little effort seems to be expended on relating the name of the shop to the merchandise offered. One must go inside and find out for oneself.

Nothing seems particularly out of place in Bahia. Across the street from the public library a record shop blares lively tunes through a loudspeaker. The brassy music fills some of the library's reading rooms, but no one seems to mind. Only one reader, a venerable sage with a flowing beard, taps to the loud rhythm with the eraser on his pencil. He flicks over the pencil like a drumstick to take notes.

A man sits on the steps of an office building. As he squeezes a ball of rubber in his hand, a toy lizard jumps out in between the feet of passers-by. Further down the street there is a huge dead rat in the gutter and a basket of flowers; seemingly there is no connection between the two.

At tables set out on the sidewalk, people pause to share a quart of beer, the standard measure in Brazil. *Guaraná,* a soda pop with a sticky apple taste, is popular too. It is made from a tropical fruit which was originally brewed into a drink by Indians living along the Tapajós river in the Amazon basin.

Sometimes crude guaraná, marketed in blocks like chocolate, is carved into figures. A common guaraná carving shows a monkey orchestra seated on a semicircular bench, shaking tambourines, strumming pear-shaped stringed instruments, and blowing horns.

The tiniest details of the streets are interesting. Ants in a long column, each ferrying a huge petal from a flower the color of orchids, march across a busy intersection, apparently undisturbed that their numbers are being decimated by rubber tires. Here and there, on the quieter suburban streets, birds hang in cages suspended from trees. It is characteristically Bahian that birds should be kept outdoors where they can be enjoyed by everybody in a more nearly natural setting, and at the same time enjoy more of life themselves.

The people in the streets are mostly Negroes, descendants of slaves imported as recently as eighty years ago. Some are tall and muscular. They have skins that range in color from a deep black, with a trace of purple, to a pale Oriental yellow. Their eyes are set apart quite far beneath their broad foreheads, giving them an attractive wide-eyed appearance.

They wear bright clothes. Some of the women do up their hair in buns, accentuating their statuesque height. Other women cover their heads with flowered squares of cloth, Bedouin style. The loose corner of the cloth switches and swatches in the wind like the tail of a horse. Occasionally, women still swathe themselves in traditional Bahian clothes, full skirts which sway like a bell, topped off by bracelets and spangles which convey the total visual impression of a pipe-smoking Creole woman of New Orleans. The younger women mostly prefer sharp uplift brassieres and tight-fitting skirts. If the skirt is so tight that it pops when she walks, so much the better.

Down a narrow lane steps a thick-lipped lady, her ebony hair combed into a crest like the comb of a rooster. She is dressed in a trim white jacket which buttons up to her neck and down to her wrists. Behind her walks a corporal in a faded uniform, the jacket darker than the pants, the cap bleached an almost pure white. In the square toward which they are headed, a truck stripped down to a cab and chassis waits on the cobblestones. The skeleton of the truck is crowned by a gilded four-poster litter beneath whose imperial splendor rests a coffin. 1347348

The men wear straw hats, with pyramid-shaped crowns suggestive of those worn by the squat men who pole burnt-out log canoes along the Amazon river. They wear their pants low on their hips, playing down their short-waistedness.

The Negroes move gracefully, from the waist down. They seem to glide effortlessly along the street, their hips taking up the jerkiness, as they set one foot ahead of another, like shock absorbers. Their shoulders seem to float, the same way they do at the animistic rite of the *Candomblé,* a shaking, swinging African ritual in which a circular dance, strange gods, and the beating of drums combine to provide a release for pagan energies.

When Sister Dulce was growing up, there were several thousand pieces of ground set aside for the practices of Candomblé; as recently as a few years ago, scholars counted five hundred. Each piece of ground is the "church" for a Candomblé congregation, a place hallowed to the awe-inspiring rites.

The tropical climate is the Bahian's best friend. The warmth of the sun precludes the necessity of heavy clothes and heated dwellings. The heavy downpours during the rainy season wash the city. The sun bakes it dry.

Were it not for the sun, it would perhaps be impossible for so much idleness to be visible in Bahia. The sun acts like a magnet in drawing people out onto the streets. The idle are as numerous as the poor. Many of the idle are children. They sit around everywhere, discarded by broken homes or born homeless.

Some idle away the day by walking around the city, looking for something to eat or something to steal. The balustraded steps of a church provide a rich backdrop for an idle boy. He watches while people come and go to pray and bask in the rich, gilded ornamentation of a cathedral. Inside there are soft scenes baked into the tiled walls, candles, and sadness brightened by the shining face of the black St. Benedict.

The young Maria Rita found ways to look behind the placid exteriors of lost children. She wasn't afraid to ask a small boy, "What are you doing, my friend?" or, "Do you have a home?" Little by little, over a lifetime, she has come to know the dank and inhospitable nooks and crannies of Bahia where the poor and homeless hide at night.

She determined very early that she wanted to help them. She was barely in her teens when she first asked her father's permission to enter the convent. He refused her request as she stood before him, her beautiful hair falling in tresses over her shoulders, a polka-dotted kerchief knotted around her neck. "You are too young, my dear. Wait for a few years and we'll discuss the matter again."

She waited, spending her time earning a teaching certificate from the Normal School of Bahia State. She requested her father's permission to become a nun twice more. The third time, he gave her his approval and blessing. At eighteen she left home to prepare to become a nun. From the convent where she trained, she sent her father the letters in her neat fine hand that today he preserves as if they were treasures. The letters are decorated with tiny flowers, to make up for the years in which she never could seem to find time to garden with her father, and to remind him to take care of his health with a vigor equal to that with which he cares for his flowers.

On August 15, 1937, at the age of twenty-three, she professed her perpetual vows as a nun in the order of the Missionary Sisters of the Immaculate Conception. Her order had been founded by two Germans—a schoolteacher and a Franciscan Missionary bishop—in 1910 at Santarem, a small community situated on the southern bank of the Amazon river.

Today, the order has approximately three hundred nuns in Brazil at thirty-six missions, many of them located in Northeast Brazil. Although nearly eighty of the nuns are German, the Mother House of the order is in Middleville, New Jersey.

To her surprise she was given the name of her mother, Dulce. It was her father's idea. She was extremely pleased to have the name, to carry on for her father's sake the glowing memory of her warm and charitable mother.

Sister Dulce was assigned to St. Anthony's Convent, which at that time was housed in a wing of the Church of Our Lady of Mercy in Bahia. The church, built in the same year as Faneuil Hall, the cradle of American liberty in Boston, is a handsome structure, a blend of baroque and rococo architecture, and of the rich traditions of the Old World as transposed in the New.

Next to the church there is a triangular plot of ground, a small green park where Sister Dulce played as a girl. From her convent she could see, as she had while a child, the serene sea that rhythmically beats out the tempo of Bahian life. According to Bahian folklore, no one knows where the sea ends, but it seemed to have a beginning in front of this church where a young nun began her career.

3

Where to Start?

HER first assignment was to teach, in the convent school, classes made up of shiny, well-brushed girls in navy blue pinafores. Try as she did, Sister Dulce was soon restless in the classroom. She didn't like the discipline which substituted for learning, the agonizing hours of penmanship and the recital of assignments committed to memory.

Scarcely six months had passed when she was called in for a scolding by her Sister Superior. "You have done it again," she said. "You have given all your students ten. Do you expect me to believe," she went on, with a long pause for a frown, "that *all* your girls earned the highest grade possible?"

The pale new nun received the admonishment placidly, with downcast eyes. She knew that she had not been much of a success at teaching world history. Somehow, the big, flat book plastered with maps and glib accounts of discoveries and wars from the beginning of recorded time bored her. It was like the haphazard plot of a novel totally unrelated to the vibrant life around her in Bahia.

"My heart isn't in teaching, I'm afraid," she replied.

The Sister Superior was indulgent. "Then what would you like to put your heart into?"

Sister Dulce was at a loss for words. She didn't have an answer. She knew only that it must be something outside of the convent walls, something that involved people. Her Superior encouraged her to think it over. Sister Dulce didn't know where to begin.

But she had to begin somewhere, so she walked around the streets of the Ribeira section near her convent, getting to know people. Since nuns are not supposed to be on the street unaccompanied, she hunted up a couple of idle young boys to be her escort. "I like to take along some youngsters wherever I go," she said. "It gives them something to do. Otherwise, who knows what deviltry they would be up to?"

It was fun exploring. She poked her head into the doorways of small businesses that were rising out of the postwar depression. There was a lumberyard where the boards were stacked like windmills. There was a boat-repair yard, called *A Bahiana* (the Bahian lady), where she paused to watch a man soldering, and there were the wharves nearby, where the fishermen with commercial boats unloaded their daily catch.

Shy by nature, she forced herself to be outgoing. This was a strain at first. Fortunately, she laughed easily. It helped to have the boys along to break the ice. She developed the habit of beginning a conversation by commenting playfully about one of the boys she had in tow, "See him, a young thief. Aren't they all young thieves! But see how this one is growing. I believe by the time he reaches manhood he may look honest."

Wherever she went, she talked to anyone who would pause long enough in his daily work to talk to her. She was an engaging sight, a young, beautiful nun dragging a youngster by either hand, like an outrigger on a canoe. She became gradually more adept at small talk, liberally sprinkling her remarks with humorous anecdotes. She earned a reputation for a quick sense of humor, "to which, we Bahians are terribly susceptible," one of her oldest admirers said.

Initially she felt a strong urge to uplift the souls of the laborers she met by encouraging them to go to church and to attend the classes she hoped to organize in the catechism. She buttonholed workers as they filed out the gates of a shoe factory, wearied by the day's work. She filled their ears with the religious platitudes which had been etched into her memory at the convent.

"Hello, John," she remembers beginning, "I hear the Lord has blessed you with a new baby."

"Yes, and with no money to feed it."

Inevitably Sister Dulce became the listener, learning how bad conditions were for the worker and his family. In the thirties, the worldwide depression, which had swept the United States a few years earlier, caused a delayed wave of despair of deep intensity throughout Brazil. Wages were low. The laboring man made barely enough to afford rice and beans, the staples of the Bahian diet, for his family. With luck he could eke out this monotonous fare with an occasional piece of fish.

At least as long as he had a job, the worker could support his family a little better than those in the alagados. But the slightest extra expense meant financial disaster for him and his family and a return to the alagados from which many of them had only recently emerged. The terrors of this drama, played out like a circus act on a high wire, impressed themselves deeply on Sister Dulce.

As in the United States, the working man was at the center of Brazil's efforts to break the grip of the depression. In the confusion of rival ideologies attempting to snatch ultimate power, a strong forceful individual, Getúlio Vargas, emerged as the leader of Brazil. Within his own vibrant personality, Vargas combined the powers of president, congress, and state governors.

By appealing to the laboring class, he gained the supporters who made it possible for him to dominate Brazilian politics for nearly a quarter of a century. The workers were enchanted by his oratory. "The Brazilian worker has never disappointed me," he said. "Diligent, a gifted learner, a remarkable doer, he knows the meaning of the word patriotism. My government is responsive to these qualities. Our labor policies do not set man against man, nor discriminate among them. Our policies unite all together, reconciling divergent views in the interest of national progress."

In spite of all his demagoguery, Vargas, reminiscent in some ways of New York's Mayor Fiorello La Guardia, retained the boyish appeal of a bright country youth from the fertile, southern cattle country of his native state of Rio Grande do Sul. He backed up his words with the first comprehensive set of labor laws in Brazilian history.

Whether they appreciated the precise significance of these laws or not, the Bahian workers were encouraged by their president's repeated exhortations to organize. Sister Dulce, never an ardent follower of politics, was interested in the president's pronouncements only to the extent that they might affect her capacity to do something for the workers.

Like most Brazilians she is scornful of the corruption and nepotism that overwhelm almost everything the government touches. She was fortunate, nonetheless, that her father was, at the time she began her career, besides being a respected dentist, a much admired and influential man in civic affairs. Through his gifts to charitable institutions, he had established himself as above the taint of corruption. The aura of his good works rubbed off on his daughter.

Without really herself appreciating the precise significance of the new labor laws, Sister Dulce encouraged the workers to organize. As she said later, "They seemed to want to." But what part could she herself as a nun play in the labor movement of Bahia?

The classes she organized in the catechism were obviously not the answer to the workers' needs. "No one came," she said. "Poor souls, they had neither the time to spare nor any interest in religious teachings." The Church, the young nun discovered "was behind the times." The great awakening of a social consciousness, as expressed in the encyclicals of the late Pope John XXIII, was thirty years off.

For her part, Sister Dulce decided to enhance the classes in the catechism with an added attraction, something closer to the spirit of the thirties. She invited some medical students she knew to drop in at the classes. They came early and sat around a plain square workbench, in the basement of a building which someone loaned to Sister Dulce.

For a half hour or so they traded medical school stories over the friendly light of a kerosene lantern. Unnoticed, at the Sister's invitation, some of the poor workers and their families filed in. They sat on the pressed earth of the basement floor, listening inquisitively to the boisterous, youthful conversation. They took in every word, like an audience at a panel show.

At the precise moment that the conversation lagged, Sister Dulce introduced her new element. She invited the students to diagnose the illnesses of those who listened seated on the floor.

"See here, my friends, how this boy has a rash on his leg. What do you suppose it could be?"

The students rose to the bait. They projected themselves into the roles of accredited doctors. They practiced what they were learning in the classroom on live patients. When they encountered symptoms they didn't recognize on the spot, they delayed giving out prescriptions until they could check their notes later at the medical school library. In a city with far too few doctors, no one seemed to mind. And filling prescriptions in Bahia is far easier than it is in the United States. Today, for example, Bahians are enthusiastically adopting penicillin, a shot of which is obtainable in any drugstore, as a remedy for the common cold.

The Sister's arrangement for medical consultation was popular. "Maybe not so clinically sterile as a hospital," one of the students, now a successful doctor, recalled, "but better than nothing." More and more people came, bringing with them sick friends and relations.

At last the young nun had found something to do. As a girl she had thought seriously about becoming a nurse. But ironically, her father had discouraged her, saying, "Nursing isn't a profession for a girl from a good family." Up until recent times, nursing in Brazil had about the same low reputation as it did in the British army of Florence Nightingale's day.

Before long Sister Dulce's superiors within her order, not wholly pleased with all the fresh obligations she had made by setting up her own charitable "organization," were unable to stop her for fear of alienating the affections of the people of Ribeira, to whom the young nun was rapidly becoming a heroine.

Never one to rest on her laurels, Sister Dulce capitalized on her own modest success. She began visiting the yellow, one-room homes of the workers with a young Bahian doctor, Renato Lobo, to take care of the sick who couldn't come to the consultations. Dr. Lobo, at that time a recent graduate of Bahia's medical school, which is the oldest in Brazil, welcomed the experience. With his help Sister Dulce was able to reach more people.

By now her example was becoming a powerful one among the laborers. Where there is, as there was at that time, so little social action, the tiniest good acts shine like the sun. Word was quickly passed around, "See Sister Dulce in time of emergency."

With more and more supporters every day, Sister Dulce had no difficulty in obtaining permission to use a local school building for regular weekend medical consultations and "classes," which were now entirely devoted to discussions of how the workers and their families could organize to take care of some of their needs.

With a little prodding from Sister Dulce and her father, who took an active interest in her career as a nun from the outset, the workers began to formulate plans for organizing themselves into a union along the lines advocated by President Vargas.

There was little experience among the workers in anything even remotely related to organization. Indeed, it was apparent from the moment the workers decided to form a union that Sister Dulce was their natural leader. She plunged into the job of union-organizing.

In her soft-spoken voice she moderated lengthy meetings, filled with the pomp and careful attention to detail that Brazilians adore. Each man was given the chance to be heard. The others listened attentively to each harangue with characteristic Brazilian politeness. The rules and purposes of the proposed union were carefully charted, haggled over, and adopted. The union was officially inaugurated in 1937. Sister Dulce's father played an important part in having the union accredited nationally.

To begin with, the workers contributed out of their meager earnings enough money to rent a small two-story building in a poor section of town. Sister Dulce helped them to convert the building into a gathering place where everyone felt welcome. Soon the building had a small library, medical clinics on scheduled days each week attended by volunteer doctors, and a group of loyal supporters.

To some, Sister Dulce's leading role in the formation of the union seemed strangely out of keeping with her clerical habit. "But not to me," said her stanch supporter, Juracy Magalhães, who had been appointed Bahia's governor by President Vargas. Governor Magalhães, presently Brazil's ambassador to the United States, helped and encouraged her at every step of the way.

Through him, Sister Dulce arranged a meeting with Vargas' successor. "How could I refuse?" the governor shrugged, as he modestly tried to minimize his contributions to Sister Dulce's work. "I am her godfather."

When she met the President, Sister Dulce wasted no time on pleasantries. She kissed his hand perfunctorily and said, "Mr. President, you are the father of my country, therefore, you are the father of my work. Many of your children need you."

Before she was through with him, the President had agreed to build a movie theater for the Workers' Union of Bahia. The theater had arisen out of a curious but logical decision on Sister Dulce's part. The workers wanted a theater. The profits from the movies, the Sister reasoned, could be turned over to the union to support social services for the workers and their families.

To understand the importance of the theater and the union, it is important to remember that the workers with whom Sister Dulce worked had had little experience in any collective undertaking. "I know it will sound silly," said one of the union's officials, "but the idea of organizing was a novelty. We were all so busy, each with his own affairs."

The community development technique which Sister Dulce employed unconsciously back in the thirties seems less original today when thousands of young men and women in the Peace Corps are trying to duplicate her feat in communities throughout Latin America. But at that time it was original indeed.

Since then the Catholic Church has participated in many programs based on this same fundamental approach: the Maryknoll Fathers, who were instrumental in setting up an extremely successful credit union program in Peru; the priests who are pushing agrarian reform in Chile; and the priests who are helping to organize labor today north of Bahia in the area of Recife.

The theater contributed to an *esprit de corps* among the workers of Bahia. It was a tangible bond among them. It developed leadership. It was the first step toward achieving a working model of the principle that in unity there is strength. Sister Dulce has quite naturally a simpler explanation for the union. "It seemed like the right thing to do."

Since it was established, the union has evolved differently from the way a comparable union in the United States might evolve. Collective bargaining and other economic goals are still a long way off in Brazil. Minimum wage laws that are on the books are unenforceable. It is common knowledge that the girls who work in one of the bigger dime stores in Bahia are paid off in a back room. Should one of them complain about not receiving the minimum wage, she would certainly lose a precious job, for which others are waiting ten-deep.

Over the years the proceeds of the theater were ploughed into several programs. A union building was erected next to the theater. Gradually, the union leaders provided the membership with social, educational and medical facilities in the building. Today the building is a beehive of activity. Besides supplying its members with medical assistance, the union provides primary schooling for children of workers. In the evenings workers themselves and their families take advantage of special self-improvement courses in typing and literacy.

The union marked its silver anniversary by issuing a small red, white, and blue pennant, proudly proclaiming the twenty-five years of its existence, 1937–1962. On the wall in the main meeting room the pictures of Pope John XXIII, Sister Dulce, and her father beamed down on the assembly.

Within the union, which today has thirty thousand members, Sister Dulce had the firm, devoted, and organized friends to whom she was to turn for help over the coming years.

The union has been a stout weapon in her hands to beat inefficient, often corrupt, governments into realizing good works on behalf of the poor. Sister Dulce had the instrument with which to embark on her next mission in the alagados.

4

The Alagados

THE World War II years found Brazil, like the rest of the world, preoccupied with ending the menace of fascism. Brazil suffered approximately five thousand casualties in the Italian campaign. During these years Sister Dulce's union began operating fairly smoothly. She herself withdrew from its active stewardship, preferring to continue working for the union as a respected adviser and arbiter, influencing only key issues on which the membership of the union found itself deadlocked.

She devoted every hour she could to the people in the alagados, which are located immediately adjacent to the Ribeira section and the growing union. Between the poor who live in the alagados and the outsider there is a solid, though intangible, wall. The wall is built of disease, ignorance, and indifference.

It takes years, as Sister Dulce learned, to get used to the alagados and to gain the confidence of the people who live there. The repulsiveness of the alagados and the people themselves is horrifying. The alagados abound in bloated bellies. The bone structures of underdeveloped bodies seem freakishly out of proportion to the flesh they enclose. Leg ulcers, great gaping sores, are commonplace. Kwashiorkor, a severe nutritional disease resulting from protein deficiency, prematurely grays or tinges with red the hair of children.

A powerful stench clings to the alagados, unrelieved by the ocean breeze that freshens the more favored seashore. Sister Dulce is accustomed to the smell. "When I'm not there, I feel as if something is missing."

She learned to live with the fever and the dysentery which are the constant companions of those who live or work in the alagados. She became as hardened as the most seasoned doctor to the ugliness of disease. One doctor, who occasionally braved the alagados with Sister Dulce, recalled one day spending hours with her, picking the maggots one by one out of the cancerous growth of a woman with a terminal illness.

This ghastly incident illustrates the enormity of the challenge with which the young nun daily grappled. Bahia's alagados are merely one manifestation of the poverty and despair which cling to a much vaster area, twice the size of Texas, where twenty-five million people live a hand-to-mouth existence.

This area is called the Brazilian Northeast. It is the bloated belly of Brazil that protrudes out into the Atlantic Ocean, closer than any other part of the South American continent to Africa. During the war the Northeast was a vital link in the chain of supply for troops fighting in North Africa and Italy. American pilots remember refueling in Natal in the Northeast before making the hop to Dakar, Africa.

To appreciate the futility that dogged the young nun's every step, it is necessary to grasp the explosive pressures that are building in this enormous area. Except for a narrow coastal strip, which is favored with a hot humid climate, the Northeast is a Brazilian dust bowl. Along the coast, the climate favors the sugar cane, cotton, and cocoa plantations which have been passed for four centuries from the hands of father to son. These plantations provide wealth for the few who live in Bahia's fine homes. For the workers, who live at the pleasure of their masters in crude shelters on the edges of the great estates, the plantations offer a livelihood approximating serfdom.

Within the interior of the Northeast, called *sertão,* there is a lengthy dry season, lasting for six months, from June to November. During this season the lands of the gigantic interior look almost like the face of the moon, pockmarked by wind and erosion, bleached out by the combined effects of sun and drought. The scrub growth in this region is called *caatinga,* mostly twisted little trees, cactuses, and prickly bushes.

It is worth describing the people who live in the sertão because they are the ones who are today filling up the alagados. The sertão was originally inhabited by pioneers who migrated from the cities of southern Brazil, especially São Paulo, to open up new lands, lands suggestive in some ways of the southwestern portion of the United States.

According to Gilberto Freyre, Brazil's foremost sociologist, "Certain tendencies in the character of the *sertanejo,* or backlander, that incline him to asceticism; a certain suspiciousness in his habits and attitudes; that air of a seminary student that he preserves all his life long; his extraordinary physical endurance; his angular Quixote-like frame, contrasting with the more rounded and sleeker figures of . . . the inhabitants of the seaboard; the purity of his blood, which only now is beginning to be contaminated with syphilis and other venereal disease—these are traits that are bound up in the most intimate manner with . . . the sertanejo. . . ." *

The image of the sertanejo, who is among the world's most rugged horsemen, exercises a strong influence on the Brazilian imagination. Since he must ride over terrain covered by

* Freyre, Gilberto, *The Masters and the Slaves* [*Casa-Grande e Senzala*], 2d English-language ed., rev. (New York, Alfred A. Knopf, 1956), pp. 399-400.

what is called a forest of thorns, he dresses himself from head to toe in leather. His curious leather hat, *chapéu de couro*, is shaped like a missile set in a saucer. When he rides he leans forward, his stomach pressed against his horse, which is itself protected against the thorns by a leather mask.

The sertanejo's dance is the *arrasta-pé*, an impetuous repetition of stamping heels and jingling spurs, to the accompaniment of an accordion or the cadence of metallic strings. The Northeasterners of the sertão are stubbornly attached to their way of life. Fierce and independent, they love the dry, clear air of the sertão and the pale blue sky.

According to the Brazilian classic, *Os Sertões*, by Euclides da Cunha, the sertanejo

... is above all else a strong individual.... His appearance, it is true, at first glance would lead one to think that this was not the case. He does not have the flawless features, the graceful bearing, the correct build of the athlete. He is ugly, awkward, stooped.... His unsteady, slightly swaying, sinuous gait conveys the impression of loose-jointedness. His normally downtrodden mien is aggravated by a dour look which gives him an air of depressing humility. On foot, when not walking, he is invariably to be found leaning against the first doorpost or wall that he encounters; while on horseback, if he reins in his mount to exchange a couple of words with an acquaintance, he braces himself on one stirrup and rests his weight against the saddle.... And if in the course of his walk he pauses for the most commonplace of reasons, to roll a *cigarro*, strike a light, or chat with a friend, he falls—"falls" is the word—into a squatting position and will remain for a long time in this unstable state of equilibrium, with the entire weight of his body suspended on his great-toes, as he sits there on his heels with a simplicity that is at once ridiculous and delightful.... But let some giddy steer up ahead stray into the tangled scrub of the caatinga, or let one of the herd at a distance become entrammeled in the foliage, and he is at once a different being and, digging his broad-roweled spurs into the flanks of his mount, he is off like a dart and plunges at top speed into the labyrinth of . . . thickets. . . . Nothing can stop him in his onward rush. Gullies, stone heaps, brush piles, thorny thickets, or riverbanks—nothing can halt his pursuit of the straying steer, for *wherever the cow goes, there the cowboy and his horse go too.* Glued to his horse's back, with his knees dug into its flanks until horse and rider appear to be one, he gives the bizarre impression of a crude sort of centaur: emerging unexpectedly into a clearing, plunging into the tall weeds, leaping ditches and swamps, taking the small hills in his stride, crashing swiftly through the prickly briar patches, and galloping at full speed over the expanse of tablelands.*

Some sixty-odd years ago, when da Cunha so described him, the sertanejo was better off than he is today. There was more space for him to graze his herds. The breakfast steaks on the table were thicker and juicier. Since then he has fallen victim to a severe population explosion and recurring drought. But essentially his spirit is unchanged.

At present there are about fifteen million backlanders who have become for the most part subsistence farmers. Typically, each farmer works a plot of land which becomes smaller and smaller as the population grows. There he raises beans and corn for his family. If he is lucky he may perhaps have a few animals, or he may work on the estate of a man who does, a man with the honorific title of colonel, who represents in the sertão what southern colonels represented in the ante-bellum south of the United States.

Each individually owned plot of land has a simple adobe-like dwelling which looks like a tiny ant hill from a distance. Whether or not the farmer can provide his family with enough to eat depends largely on whether it rains enough when his crops need rain. Frequently, it doesn't rain at the right time.

---

* Da Cunha, Euclides, *Rebellion in the Backlands* [*Os Sertões*] (Chicago, University of Chicago Press, 1944), pp. 89-91.

Then both farmer and animals grow lean and the farmer anxiously watches the sky. About once every decade, the Northeast has to endure a devastating one-to-three-year drought.

There is luck involved. Here and there, a sudden rain will fall even in times of drought. At once the area so favored will blossom forth with a deep tropical green. But most are not so lucky. Drought, combined with an increasingly intense pressure for good land, forces farm families reluctantly off the land. As harsh as their life is, under normal conditions the Northeasterners accept its asperities with hard work and an indomitable will to survive.

The climatic moment, when drought and the prospect of starvation force a Northeastern family off the sere land, is among the most moving migration stories in the world. It has been the subject of a string of novels, legends, and movies that appeal very deeply to the Brazilian consciousness.

There is a more or less constant stream of humanity, even during good years, people forced off the land and migrating in waves to the coast and the big cities like Fortaleza, Recife, and Bahia. When the backlanders arrive in the city they are recognizable to all. Something about the coarseness of their manners, their clothes tattered to shreds, and their parched physiques gives them away. The backlander's adjustment to the city is a theme for a whole genre of Brazilian jokes which has its origin in humorous episodes from their tragic lives.

Like other coastal cities, Bahia cannot absorb them. There are not enough jobs to go around as it is, to say nothing of jobs for unskilled and uneducated backlanders. What's more, there is no remedy in sight. Feeble efforts by the Brazilian government have fallen far short of reducing the number of homeless and jobless migrants. "They have traded one bondage for another," said former Brazilian President Café Filho. "In the sertão they suffered the *miséria morta* (dead misery), unseen and forgotten; in the city they suffer the *miséria viva* (living misery), seen by everybody, a national disgrace."

His comment points up an important distinction. The migrant from the sertão is not the dreg of society normally associated with city slums. Like the majority of the fifty-five million people who over the next ten years will be added to Latin America's major cities, he is frequently an energetic element of society. He is the victim of a steady drop in per capita agricultural productivity which has been experienced in Latin America over recent years. His migration is in part attributable to the price that must be paid for uncontrolled population expansion, in part to medical advances not offset by economic progress, and in part to a new social consciousness broadcast by communications media to remote areas of the continent.

Only starvation ultimately was capable of forcing him from a hard-working life on the land. His tragedy lies in the inability of underdeveloped societies, like Brazil's, to provide new opportunities for him to equip himself for a place in modern industry. Within the vast area of the sertão, the average per capita income hovers around one hundred dollars per year. In Bahia, approximately one-quarter of all those employed are employed as domestics.

Away from their natural homes and the only way of life they have ever known, the backlanders become a burden to society. They have nowhere to turn. But they stay on in Bahia, hoping vainly to find a job, and rapidly being sucked like water down a drain into the sewer of the alagados.

Soon hope gives way to brute urges—to eat, to sleep, to exist. The spectacle of their stout country spirits being broken by the alagados is a pitiful sight. The backlanders become degraded, as Sister Dulce learned—degraded physically, socially, and spiritually.

During the years that she spent so much time there, Sister

Dulce learned to sympathize with the causes of life in the alagados. As a girl she had learned only about the symptoms, the beggar who stopped by her gate to ask for a meal. Now she was knocking at the hovels of beggars, trying to encourage people who were by and large beyond encouragement.

She learned that privacy within the alagados is impossible. Few of the one-room hovels house families for long. Instead, they house random collections of people, held together, if at all, by a woman past child-bearing. Driven by some primitive instinct, the woman puts out something to eat when she can. She is much like a cat offering her drying teats to a litter of rapacious kittens. It isn't her fault if she can't do better. She has been discarded by one, perhaps several, men, who used her as long as she had something physical to offer. Soon, the woman, worn down by suckling her own children, is exhausted.

Over and over again Sister Dulce's ears were filled to overflowing with tales of woe. A small girl, whose mother had died, came to Sister Dulce for help. The girl had twenty-four brothers and sisters—none of them by the same father as herself. Sister Dulce helped the youngster find a job as a domestic in the home of a prosperous friend, where she learned by observation the meaning of the words family and father. Without some experience of these words it would have been difficult for the girl to have become a Christian.

Another girl, scarcely past puberty, came to Sister Dulce, breathless. "The poor girl, the poor thing. Her father threatened to kill her with a knife if she refused his advances," said Sister Dulce. It took months of constant companionship for Sister Dulce to quell the girl's fear and trembling.

As hardened as she became to the sight of physical disease, Sister Dulce couldn't lose her sensitivity to human suffering. "It hurt to watch her," said one of her friends from the labor union, who has given her a little sack of coffee for the poor every week or so for twenty years. Sometimes, Sister Dulce, moved by a personal tragedy, broke under the strain into a quiet sobbing.

Her sadness, curiously enough, was a bridge to the poor, who almost never cry. They saw in her an expression of what was in their hearts. Her tears were as much a release for them as they were for her.

And gradually, over the years, Sister Dulce, by making herself always available, earned their confidence. She spent every hour she could in the alagados, helping people one at a time. Indeed, she became such a familiar sight in the alagados that her name became synonymous with charity. When the other nuns in her order began working there, they were hailed as "Sister Dulce"—a reaction that inspired some resentment among them.

Sister Dulce developed a singular skill at getting across to the poor. She became adept at holding up both ends of a conversation that otherwise would have bogged down completely, owing to ignorance. She asked a small boy, for example, "What do you do every day?" She found he was unable to answer because he couldn't handle the abstract concept of "day." She quickly filled in the answer for him.

He nodded. The conversation went on.

She applied herself to mastering the idiom of gesticulation which is frequently a more precise means of expression in the alagados than words. To say: "It doesn't matter," one slaps the back of one hand against the palm of the other in rapid alternating succession. To refer to a thief, one twists the thumb of the right hand against the palm of the left. To express satisfaction at one's good luck, one presses the earlobe between the thumb and index finger of the right hand.

For the moment the job of Christianizing Bahia's poor seemed to the maturing nun to be beyond the reach of human accomplishment. "Our job is to feed and clothe them first," she said. "Only after they have enough to eat are they able to partake like sensible Christians of the Holy Gospels."

As it was, even simple ceremonies became complex affairs when performed on behalf of those in the alagados. The last rites for a dying man lucky enough to be within reach of a priest stretched on endlessly. "He had lived with ten or eleven women," Sister Dulce said. "He couldn't remember their names. He didn't even remember the names of his own children." The concept of sin was alien to his mind. It had to be explained to him on his deathbed.

The ignorance of the poor, almost all of them nominal Catholics, was and is appalling. A priest who worked with Sister Dulce told the story of a man who asked him after the Mass, "Father, I recognize St. Anthony [the patron saint of Sister Dulce's work], but who is that other saint with his hands nailed to the cross?"

Religion among the poor was a mixture of African and Christian rituals. Thousands went to practice the shaking, dancing, frantic voodoo rite of the Candomblé. Women of all ages swirled around for hours in a huge circle, throwing up their hands, tossing back their heads, and invoking the pagan deities brought by their ancestors to the New World in the holds of slave ships.

In the midst of such universal ignorance and futility, where healing frequently served to prolong the misery of existence, Sister Dulce steeled herself to thinking in the present tense. She developed a remarkable power of concentration which she learned to direct, like the point of a needle, at the specific malady to which she was attending.

Nonetheless, she was gnawed by a desire to do more. Without some permanent place to care for the sick and house the homeless, she was driven to nurse them in their own environment, filthy slums where many of the social and physical illnesses she was trying to cure were directly traceable to un-liveable conditions and poor diets. Fortunately, she was sustained by her own frantic pace of activity. Otherwise, the hopelessness of life in the alagados might have overwhelmed her.

5

The Clinic

THAT the alagados would abound in errands of mercy for a charitable nun is scarcely surprising. The alagados thrive on misery, even as they thrive on garbage. Someone has suggested that the easiest way of doing away with the alagados would be to do away with the garbage deliveries which create them. But this would ignore the nature of the alagados, for once the garbage has been solidified, the land actually acquires value.

The land which was settled earlier, along the back edge of the alagados, nearest the center of the peninsula, now has some shops and stores, modest ones to be sure. Nonetheless, this land which was covered with alagados a few years ago has acquired some value for merchants capable of turning a profit from those in the alagados.

A cleric, who wishes to remain anonymous because of what he feels is the unorthodoxy of his views, pointed out that, in his opinion, God's purpose in the alagados was to demonstrate that out of evil can come good. Otherwise, life in the alagados would seem to be an exercise in futility.

It was not long before Sister Dulce was in danger of being defeated by the alagados, by the demands which increased in intensity like the sun's rays at midday. Each hour brought calls for help. Some poor wretch vomiting blood, in the final throes of tuberculosis, would send for her. Some woman, whose husband had deserted her and a large family, would block her path. Sister Dulce's strength was being rapidly spent.

She acknowledges that at this point in her life she felt as though she was on a treadmill, trying to keep pace but losing ground all the time. She developed a cough but fortunately not tuberculosis. She could not control her impatience and her anxiety. She was, she says, on the threshold of desperation. She seriously wondered whether she had been forsaken by God.

Then, unexpectedly, towards the end of a long day, Sister Dulce came upon a small boy suffering from fever, who changed the course of her life. She wanted to do something for the boy, huddled in the doorway of an abandoned building. But she had no place to take him.

As she kneeled to examine him, she prayed. In answer to her prayers, she remembered an empty house near the convent. She carried the boy in her arms to the house. She broke the lock. Without debating the propriety of her action, she picked up the boy and carried him inside.

She spread out a mat for the boy to lie on while she consoled him with kind words. Night was coming on fast, so she hurried out to buy a small lantern to keep the boy company. She stopped at the house of a priest whom she knew on the way back from the marketplace. The priest's sister gave her a bowl of hot chicken soup for the hungry boy.

Within a few days, Sister Dulce had a "clinic." There were five patients in the house. Unfortunately, they all died, including the small boy, who succumbed to the ravages of advanced tuberculosis and malnutrition. Of all the thousands of patients for whom she has cared, the small boy, hollow-eyed, puny, advanced in years in his capacity to suffer out the pains of death, impressed himself most vividly on her memory. The thought of him still leads her on, like a torch in the night.

There is something about the appearance of a single neglected child which poignantly brings home the importance of thousands of similarly neglected children. A prematurely born baby, well endowed with hair, with lines, and with an ashen complexion that suggests great age, conveys some of this feeling; but he will live.

The child which Sister Dulce beheld would not. The spectacle of the dying child transfixes the eyes of the beholder. The tilt of his head and the sparseness of his hair suggest a crown of thorns and the attitude of Christ on the cross. It is a feeling which defies distance and words, and it is curious, but the sight of such a child inspires the deepest feelings of faith, not only in God, but in the human race as well.

The boldness with which man undertakes his journey, the fragile thread upon which he clings to life, the promise of fulfillment denied—are all quite starkly revealed in a sudden nearing to the secret of the universe. In Sister Dulce's life, where time to care for one child has always had to yield to the exigencies of caring for many, that one dying boy was, she said, God's way of telling her what she must do.

In the process of caring for him Sister Dulce had become a confirmed housebreaker. She "admitted" her patients to five empty tumble-down houses, all in a row on the same deserted street. One by one she filled each room with her patients. At length the owner of the houses found out about her clandestine acquisition of his property. He ordered her and her patients to vacate the premises.

But Sister Dulce's mercy was contagious. The other nuns in her order, mostly women advanced in years, encouraged her. With their help and the help of some appreciative ex-patients, Sister Dulce carried the equipment she had accumulated in the five houses—sixty straw mats, five kerosene lamps, five buckets, five dippers, and five slop pails—to a new location.

The new location was the shelter provided by the twenty stone arches that support an ancient viaduct which leads up to the lovely Bahian Basilica of Bomfim (meaning "happy end"). There, under the arches—which make the foreground of a beautiful picture postcard view of the Basilica with its red-tiled roof and its twin tiled spires—Sister Dulce set up her clinic.

The arches, fifteen to twenty feet deep, would, she reasoned, provide protection from the rain and the blistering tropical sun. With scraps of tin and packing cases, she and her helpers sealed off each of the wards under the arches from the prying eyes of passers-by. But before long Sister Dulce was ousted again, this time by the health authorities for creating a public eyesore next to a famous tourist attraction. "And they were justified," she said recently, without a trace of bitterness, "we were."

Meanwhile, the ranks of her loyal accomplices had swelled. They helped her beat down the doors of a deserted market, a big square structure with an ample courtyard, to make room for Sister Dulce's patients—a baby abandoned on a trash heap, a man with open gangrenous wounds found nearly dead on the waterfront, a little girl with a raging fever left to wander the streets crying.

But it was only a few months before she was ordered to move on. Once again, everything had to be picked up and carried to a new location, this time to the alley next to the convent. Crude, lean-to shacks were constructed against the convent wall. Scarcely were they completed when they were filled with patients.

The Sisters agreed to add the convent's chicken coop to Sister Dulce's domain. The night before they moved into the coop, everyone in the clinic had chicken, a rare treat. The next night, after a hard day's work with a shovel, a broom, or a rake, they looked with pride at the converted coop and saw "the first sign of better days to come." Holes had been dug into the earth next to each mat-covered, wood-plank bed. By each hole there was a pile of clean sand from the beach to "flush" the toilets.

Still, makeshift was the word that most adequately described the clinic. The malnutrition and other illnesses that could be cured by improved care were treated. Her friend from the days when she made the rounds of the workers' homes, Dr. Renato Lobo, came, whenever he could find time, to help with more serious illnesses. He brought with him other Brazilian doctors who wanted to help. The doctors helped fill out the papers for some with serious, though not incurable, diseases so that they could be jammed ahead on waiting lists for Bahia's hopelessly overcrowded public medical facilities.

In all, the clinic was a sorting house, where the hopeless could die in peace and expect a proper burial, where the seriously sick had at least the slim hope of admittance to a proper medical facility and where the homeless destitute had a home. Above all, the clinic was a place where those afflictions that could be cured by love and kindness were cured.

It was a step higher from the old way. Here at least the poor were not prey to folk remedies: the resin from a tree to heal wounds, the smoking of tobacco to heal venereal disease, and cakes soaked in water to cure worms in children.

It was better than standing in the local pharmacy where, according to free-wheeling Brazilian custom, one can get a shot in the arm without a prescription. The poor still line up in an alagados pharmacy, clutching in their dirty fists enough money for a precious shot of penicillin from a dirty needle. Not long ago, a man died after a shot in the local

pharmacy; his contorted body fell and blocked the doorway.
The "pharmacist" merely pushed the body out into the street
to await the arrival of the health authorities and closed his
pharmacy for the rest of the day.

Here the shrill, desolate cry of *miséria viva*—the awful
symbol of Brazil's forgotten poor—gave way to a prayer, a
pill, a hope. Here a woman in labor could give birth on a
bed instead of on the floor of her grubby hut, unattended,
in many instances, until it was too late.

The clinic was a light, attracting the poor like flies. The
needs of the clinic were growing every day. The wherewithal
to feed and care for sixty to seventy patients had to be
begged, meals had to be served, doctors prevailed upon for
free visits to urgent cases, medicines begged, and a hundred
other items that go hand in hand with the operation of a
public facility had to be taken care of.

Sister Dulce was the pivotal point for the satisfaction of all
these needs. She became obsessed with filling the needs of
her patients. She became, as she is today, in the words of a
Brazilian admirer, "the shortest path between my money
and the poor. She is like an army of blind men with cups."

"She became unbearable," said another admirer, a woman,
who has been acquainted with her since childhood. "And
who could resist her? That smile, that charm, that willful-
ness and disregard for anything except 'her poor'—all hidden
behind the flowing robes of a nun."

In Sister Dulce's eyes everything she could lay her hands
on had its use—a liter of gas, some old silverware, a broken
chair—all are acceptable currency. Indeed, the immediacy
with which she converts a gift into a useful purpose is an
important characteristic of Sister Dulce's work.

Person-to-person charity has a long tradition in Bahia. As
it is practiced in Bahia, charity frequently involves both the

giver and the receiver directly. Charity is giving a needy person something on the spot, perhaps buying a hungry man a meal at a restaurant and then sitting down to eat with him.

Organized charities with boards of administrators and collections on fixed dates do not appeal to the Bahian insistence on personal involvement. Brazilians generally are suspicious of organizations, perhaps because their own government, which plays a pervasive role in both public and private matters, is so notoriously corrupt and unable to inspire public confidence.

Although her methods might sound haphazard, they work in Bahia. Sister Dulce is a broker converting everything she can lay her hands on into something connected with her charitable ends. "Whenever I see her coming down the street, with those boys in tow, I automatically button my wallet in my back pocket," said a Bahian businessman. A struggling artist remembers when Sister Dulce crossed his path. "I gave her a painting," he said. "It was all I had. And the next thing you know, she had raffled it off. She made more money off it than I have ever got for a single painting."

It was not long before Sister Dulce had mastered the technique of supporting her clinic. She developed an intelligence network that included nearly everybody in Bahia, rich and poor alike. With this information she knew who had something to give away practically before the person himself did. She learned which businessmen had made money recently, and where she could fill this or that need in a hurry.

She was restless again. She wanted to do more. At this moment she remembered her old friend, Governor Magalhães. He had been reelected to office. When she visited him, he encouraged her, "Be realistic, my dear. Consolidate your gains."

"But, my godfather," she said, "I need some land."

"What in the world for?" he replied with amazement.

"To build a hospital," she replied.

The governor promised her nothing, only that he would indeed pay a visit to her clinic in the chicken coop. That was enough, and Sister Dulce knew it.

CHAPTER

6

St. Anthony Sanitarium

W HEN he was discussing his association with
Sister Dulce recently, Governor Magalhães suddenly turned
and pointed to the hair on his arm, saying, "You see, even
today I can't think about her without my hair standing on
end."

It was not long before the visit to the chicken-coop clinic
worked its spell on him, or, as he expressed it, "the immensely
sad picture of an abject heap of human beings kept alive
through God's grace and the Holy Sister Dulce."

Capable, business-like, famed throughout Brazil for his
insistence on punctuality, Governor Magalhães looked for
a way to help. Shortly thereafter, at his urging, the state
government deeded to Sister Dulce the title to a piece of
land next to the Workers' Club of Bahia.

There in May 1959 Sister Dulce called together her friends
for an important announcement. She started by reminding
them that she didn't have a cent to her name. She shrugged
off her financial embarrassment by saying, "If it's God's work,
God will help." Then she dropped the bombshell. She said
that she had just signed a $100,000 contract for the construc-
tion of a building to be called the Albergue Santo Antônio.

Literally, the words mean "St. Anthony Sanitarium." Sister
Dulce intended that the Albergue would be a clearing house
for patients from the alagados on the way to other hos-

pitals, and a temporary home for those who were abandoned or destitute.

As if he had already not done enough, Sister Dulce needled the governor to do more. She hinted to him privately that people were up in arms over the corruption of the state-run lottery, called *jôgo de bicho*. "What a good way for you to become popular, my godfather," she said, "by turning over the proceeds from the lottery to me."

The governor, eager to make his new administration popular with the people, saw the wisdom of her counsel. He arranged to have the proceeds from the troublesome, politically dangerous lottery divided among the charitable activities in Bahia. Sister Dulce's share was two hundred thousand cruzeiros, approximately two hundred dollars a month. With this sum Sister Dulce hoped to pay the upkeep of the Albergue. Little did she know how far short of her needs this sum would be.

Construction began. The workers, all of them belonging to Sister Dulce's union, put in long, hard hours. In February 1960 a 150-bed, three-story building opened its doors to those in need of food, shelter and medical care.

The construction cost was paid off in full ninety days later. Even to those closest to Sister Dulce, the way she financed the total cost of the Alburgue remains a closely guarded secret. When asked about it, she replies, with a merry gleam in her eyes, "Some friends helped. You might say we sent the bill to God."

Scarcely had the Albergue been completed when Sister Dulce was once again at the governor's palace, insisting that the governor give her the piece of marshy ground across from the Albergue. "I need more land—land for the homeless, those too well to be in the Albergue and too weak to take care of themselves."

It was typical of Sister Dulce. "Filling one need always

creates a dozen more," she said. "And we had to clear out the Albergue," she added, "so there would be some room for the sick. It's so hard, so impossible, to sort out the sick from the poor. The healthy people in the alagados, it seems, are just a handful."

The governor was angry with her. "Be realistic," he urged her again, "don't overextend yourself." He was at the time, he remembers, especially piqued at the way Sister Dulce barged into the palace, interrupting whatever was going on so that she could promote her work before the governor and his visitors. "She didn't let anyone slip through her net," the governor said. "I don't believe we had a single important visitor to Bahia in the years I was governor who didn't meet her in my palace. It made me mad sometimes to have her waving blank checks in front of everybody, much as I admire her."

Sister Dulce prevailed. The governor arranged for the state to give her the land across the street from the Albergue. Her truck-driver friends raised the land to street level by bringing loads of fill during their off hours. There she and her friends built some ramshackle buildings to house the homeless.

Out behind the Refuge, as it is called, a drunk knows that he is free to writhe through the awful terror of delirium tremens undisturbed, except perhaps for a stray dog tinkling through a heap of flattened tin cans. When the man is once more in control of himself, he is free to leave without being lectured at. He merely rubs his eyes, shakes himself all over like a dog with fleas, and wanders off. Perhaps he will get drunk all over again.

This bald ground lies between a tottering board fence and the Refuge itself. The Refuge is a long, low line of sheds that lean against one another for support. One of the sheds is called the Women's Refuge. It is generally filled to capacity, all ten beds, with women who have for one reason or another fallen on hard times. Some of the women are incurably sick with diseases which are judged to be noncommunicable. But the majority are women who no longer have a useful place in society, such as it is in the alagados.

The women's individual histories are eloquent testimony to the cruelty of life in the alagados. One had been turned out of her hovel after the death of her husband by a strange family that moved in on her, according to the law of the jungle. Helpless, without a friend to whom to turn, she heard about this small corner of the earth where she could enjoy safety and something to eat. Three other women are victims of desertion. Their husbands had left in search of work several years ago and never returned. The women earn their room and board at the Refuge by doing laundry and caring for stray children.

Near the women's shed there is a shed devoted to storage. Fresh white sacks lean against the walls filled with precious staples, such as flour obtained through Caritas, the worldwide Catholic Relief Service, or through the U.S. Food for Peace program.

Sister Dulce is high on the list of recipients of both these organizations. She is proud of the snapshot she asked someone to take, showing the small bakery her helpers constructed to serve the Albergue's bread needs. The sign lettered on the side of the oven reads "Forno da Aliança para o Progresso [Oven of the Alliance for Progress]." Sister Dulce shows this picture to visiting officials, explaining: "This is the first oven in Brazil to make bread out of Food for Peace grain." Whether it's true or not, Sister Dulce makes good use of foodstuffs that come her way. The dust does not accumulate on the sacks in her storage shed.

In front of the storehouse an old woman busies herself ripping up old rags. She rips carefully, slowly, making them into sanitary napkins. Her work, the baking, and the laundry hung

out on the drooping clotheslines tell the story of an afternoon's activities in the Refuge.

Every morning Sister Dulce or one of her helpers shoos
out the capable people in the Refuge. She drives them out
like a hen a brood of chicks. "They must work," she says,
"if they can." She gives them things to sell: cigars, fruit,
combs, and a miscellany of other items donated to her work
the day before.

This is in itself no mean accomplishment. She is never
wholly successful. Most of the people in the Refuge are
strangers to working independently. A man given five combs
to sell on the street, nodded appreciatively and with seeming
comprehension. Then he went around to the back of the
Refuge and napped the whole day. A boy given some fruit
walked on down the street and ate it himself. No amount of
sternness on Sister Dulce's part can galvanize the poor into
action for long. So many of them appear to be dazed or shell-
shocked, totally oblivious to incentive.

In and around the Refuge there are always children at
play. Some belong to families resting up temporarily in the
Refuge en route from the Northeast to southern Brazil, to
the great industrial city of São Paulo where the chances of
finding a job are pretty good for those who can stand the long
trip. But most of the children in the Refuge have no parents.
Sister Dulce or her helpers found them on the street, abandoned by their parents. Some of the children themselves deserted their parents as soon as they were old enough to get
out from underfoot.

Within the Refuge there are always a few beggars or bums.
Every night men hang around trying to get in. It is so
simple to be admitted that it is only natural to find some
drones. The old faithful retainer who watches the gate swing
open and shut with people's comings and goings has the most
rudimentary of instructions: Send anyone who wants to get

into the Refuge across the street to ask the permission of any staff member at the Albergue. The reason for this requirement is simple—to keep out of the Refuge those with communicable diseases.

As a rule, each person admitted to the Refuge must take a bath before eating and finding his own place to sleep in the sheds. There are never enough beds. But there is always something to keep the person off the ground, a board or a gunnysack or something. Except for an occasional chronic freeloader, no one is ever turned away. Even then, a good fresh excuse will get him in.

At night, usually twice a week, Sister Dulce is out, in violation of the rules of her order, adding to her problems. Accompanied by a policeman or a lay volunteer she drives around in a pickup truck scouting for the homeless. On one such occasion, according to a recent eyewitness account, she came upon "an ancient blind man who clutched his pathetic belongings suspiciously until convinced that she really meant to give him shelter and food. Huddled in a doorway nearby was a cripple whose face bore an expression of dazed disbelief as she tenderly helped him towards the truck."

Sister Dulce has a special affection for those poor souls who must sleep in doorways along the sidewalks of downtown Bahia. On any night the sight of figures lying across the thresholds of office buildings is a familiar one. The people she finds in doorways are the most difficult of all to integrate into society, according to her, because they have lost all hope.

The doorways of churches are no exception. She always finds someone sleeping in the grand wide doorway of the golden church of São Francisco. There is a special poignancy in the fact that the massive doors to this church are securely bolted against potential robbers except for a few hours during the week. At night as many as four or five people sleep on the church's broad thresholds, worn down by the passage of hundreds of thousands of the faithful.

There one night she found a woman in the final stages of pregnancy, her bed a newspaper, her pillow a hard little bundle held together by a bit of colored rag. Inside the Church, members of a Franciscan order of monks were neatly arranging the stamps they sell to tourists in see-through envelopes. One of the most popular stamps portrays Marshal Rondon, the Indian's friend, who issued the famous order, "Be killed but never kill," to all his subordinates in the Indian service. As in a mighty fortress, the monks bend over their labors, while the frail nun picks up the homeless from their doorstep.

She brings back with her to the Refuge all the people she finds on the streets. The Refuge houses a mixed lot of humanity, the only common denominator being need. Unbeknown to Sister Dulce, the Refuge has on occasion harbored criminals. The police are very polite in asking her permission to have a look around, which she readily grants. Once the International Police, the men from Interpol, found a desperately wanted man there.

The Refuge also encloses a little extra space for Sister Dulce's motor pool, three vehicles—the old green truck given to her by the City of Bahia; the Chevrolet carryall paid for by an American doctor's friends in Waukegan, Illinois; and, until it exploded and burned, the Volkswagen bus. The vehicles are worked to death, taking off on all sorts of errands in response to urgent, spur-of-the-moment requests.

Across the wide Avenue Luiz Tarquinio stands the back door of the Albergue. People have a decided preference for the back door. At almost any hour there are people standing around in a tiny patio protected from the direct rays of the afternoon sun by the roof of the Albergue. The poor linger in the patio in preference to the waiting room in front where there are two long benches.

There is something about standing around that seems to appeal to the timorous needy. It is informal. One is less conspicuous, less committed than if one were to be seated on a waiting-room bench. One old woman, who waited all day to see Sister Dulce, walked off for no apparent reason when she saw Sister Dulce coming. Not infrequently, a baby will die in his mother's arms before the mother gets up enough gumption to call her child to the attention of Sister Dulce. "They wait so long," wailed Sister Dulce. "They don't know how serious an illness is. They are so stubbornly patient."

The poor who stand around have an air of detachment. Only furtively do they glance around to look at others like themselves. There is little conversation, except for an occasional quiet word exchanged between a mother and her child. Even children are unnaturally quiet.

The silence is pregnant with despair. Each person seems totally preoccupied with his own hope for relief—one from the agony of an abscessed tooth, another from the responsibility of caring for a mentally retarded child. "There are so many children," says Sister Dulce. "There are too many children, and yet they are always having more."

The casualness of the Albergue engenders a confidence among the poor, an absence of the self-consciousness they feel at other public facilities. The Albergue is absolutely free from any bureaucratic officials or nuisances. There are no forms to fill out. Paper work and bustling efficiency, the bane of many hospitals run under Bahian governmental auspices, have no foothold here.

Not all of the people attracted to the Albergue are sick. Some come simply to be onlookers, to watch, vacant-eyed, the drama of their own lives unroll. Others feel good, as one expressed it, by being near Sister Dulce.

Sister Dulce has a friendly word for everybody. She doesn't seem to mind the staring eyes. She moves around from group to group, finding the sick ones. She listens to any story, no matter how preposterous. Once in a while she traps herself by taking both sides of the conversation and coming to unwarranted conclusions. A woman leading an old man by the hand recently engaged Sister Dulce's attention.

"What's the matter?" she asked.

Silence. The woman, like so many of the poor, couldn't express whatever it was that was on her mind.

"Is he blind?" asked Sister Dulce, pointing to the man. Silence again. "Oh, poor man," Sister Dulce went on. The woman nodded. The old man seemed to concur by giving a look of despair.

Sister Dulce led the couple hurriedly to the doctor, who was in the midst of examining a boy with something stuck in his eye. "Doctor, he's blind," she said pointing to the old man.

The doctor held up two fingers and asked the old man, "How many?" Without blinking the man replied, "Two." Shrugging his shoulders, the doctor returned to the boy.

Later on that same day, the woman, after a long wait, once again got the attention of the doctor. "Thanks to the Lord, he's not blind, Doctor. He's suffering from the beginnings of a heart attack."

The doctor, experienced in the devious ways of his poor patients, was not taken in. Obviously, the woman, with the old man's connivance, wanted to get him into the hospital where he could enjoy good meals and live on Sister Dulce's relief.

The Albergue is alive with such daily intrigue. Much of the staff work revolves around sorting out the genuinely sick from the psychosomatic cases, and discouraging people who are trying to lay their hands on free medicine and treatment for which they could afford to pay.

Recently a young boy showed up at the Albergue with a note from one of the directors of the labor union next door, which Sister Dulce founded. The note asked the doctor to give the boy some "red-blooded" vitamin pills. The doctor wrote, "No," on the note and sent it back with the boy. In the doctor's opinion, the director was well enough off to buy his own vitamins. "The ones we have are for the poor."

Next day a different boy showed up, his note requesting "red-blooded" vitamins for a destitute man unable to come to the Albergue himself. Although the note was written in a different hand, the doctor wasn't fooled.

At the moment he was examining the contents of a shipment of medical supplies which had been sent by a charitable organization in the United States. One carton had broken open. The contents of several different kinds of pill boxes had become hopelessly mingled. The doctor filled an envelope with an assortment of pills of different sizes and colors and gave it to the boy saying, "Tell whoever it is who needs the pills not to worry about the difference in size and color. Tell him to take one pill a day."

The front door of the Albergue faces on a square yard, enclosed with chain-link fencing. Over the door there is a gaudy tilework representation of St. Anthony, who looks cherubic and curiously out of place. Inside the door there are the benches where patients may wait but don't.

A meandering corridor winds through the hospital, tying together an assortment of facilities. Among them are the emergency room where volunteer doctors from Bahia and the United States hold *ambulatórios*, scheduled hours for consultation, usually two to three times a week. During ambulatórios, patients' needs are tended assembly-line style, one of the few compromises between the Albergue and systematic medical care.

The undisputed mistress of the emergency room is a large, strong woman, Edna Morreira de Nascimento. "Big Edna," as she is called, has been working for Sister Dulce for four years. She began working the night shift, sitting half awake in the emergency room, alert for nocturnal emergencies. Then, later, she was given the task of building the hospital's blood bank, which is made possible by the donations of blood by sailors at the local naval base.

At present Edna, in addition to her numerous other activities, works the dayshift as the chief on-duty staff member. She lends a hand during operations too. She is not yet a registered nurse. From a poor family, Edna never had an opportunity to become one. Although her duties at the Albergue leave her little extra time, this she spends boning up to pass the stiff exams to become a registered nurse.

Next to the emergency room is the pharmacy which, thanks to donations from the United States, is well stocked. Out in the hallway, next to the pharmacy, there is an X-ray machine which is hard to keep supplied with film because there is so much tuberculosis in the alagados.

Further on down the corridor is the laboratory. A thin girl, looking as scared as a deer on the first day of hunting season, manages the lab. Her name is Iracy. She is the sole source of support for eleven people in her family, who live in one of the worst sections of the alagados. As if this were not enough, Iracy attends school in the afternoon to learn, like Edna, more of the theory associated with her work.

Across the hall there are other facilities: the main kitchen, the blood bank, and the morgue. When the Albergue is filled to overflowing with patients, Sister Dulce sets up cots in the morgue and tells new arrivals that it is an annex to the tuberculosis ward.

The pediatrics section consists of four rooms: a play room, two wards with beds for thirty children, and an isolation unit. A few of the children have been in pediatrics for years. The most memorable is the smiling blue-eyed Ricardo, his arms and legs atrophied because of the terrible effects of thalidomide. In spite of his unhappy history and bleak future, he seems happy enough.

They say his mother was about to poison him when he was an infant. There seemed little point in letting him live. She was reaching for a newspaper in which to wrap Ricardo for deposit in the garbage when she saw a picture of Sister Dulce. The reminder of the Sister's good name made her change her mind. She brought her baby to the nun. For several years he has been the brightest face in the children's ward. Sister Dulce makes it a point to show him off to visitors. "He may die young but he will die happy," she says.

The corridor continues and passes through a small garden where at one time boys hammered together coffins for those who died in the Albergue. Now the coffin-making has been relegated to a carpentry shop hidden away in a room off the garden.

Off the garden too, there is a dark room where lepers wait before being taken to the leprosarium in the interior of the State of Bahia. Another small room has been converted into a dentist's office. There, Aluisio, Sister Dulce's devoted brother, takes care of patients' most pressing dental problems.

Aluisio has an agreeable, good-natured face. He enjoys telling about how he learned to speak English during the Second World War. He worked as a dentist evenings at Ipiritanga airfield, a base built by the U.S. for the use of flyers shuttling planes across the Atlantic to Africa. Aluisio enters cautiously into conversations about politics; he has never been known to express his true feelings to Americans.

One suspects that he dislikes Americans, but it would be hard to say just why.

In the shaded garden patients convalesce. There is the omnipresent sound of a mop; someone is always, it seems, swabbing down the floors. Further on down the corridor there is a tiny chapel where a visiting priest says Mass for the sisters every morning.

Across the hall from the Chapel is Sister Dulce's office. It is a small, boxlike room with a desk, a swivel chair, and a squat telephone table. On top of the desk there is a little plant stand, the gift of some wellwisher, with a few scraggly plastic flowers.

On one wall hangs a picture of Jesus holding the world in his hands. Beneath the world there is a simple verse:

> The sun makes the wheat
> The wheat makes the bread
> And the wheat that makes unleavened bread
> Makes the sun shine in your heart.

On another wall there is an idyllic scene, a black and white reproduction of a painting showing a circle of white-gowned, chubby girls dancing around a fountain in a sylvan paradise. This vision of mythical beatitude seems stridently out of harmony with the Albergue.

Behind Sister Dulce's desk is a tall window. Curious boys come and sit on the window ledge and eavesdrop on the conversation whenever Sister Dulce has a visitor. This she doesn't mind as long as they sit quietly. But if they make noise, she shoos them off the ledge and lowers the opaque window, foregoing the wisp of fresh air which is blown into the office and the glimpse of a green-breasted parakeet, one of two birds in a cage hung from a tree outside.

The men's wards, accommodating about eighty patients, are on the second floor. Double-decker beds are arranged close together. Soon each patient knows his neighbors' problems as intimately as his own.

There is a more or less constant bustling around. Patients visit one another a great deal. The less sick perform as sort of conscript nurses, bringing glasses of water and food to those unable to get out of bed. The unconventional atmosphere, reminiscent of the pointless amiability one might expect to find at a crowded beach, contributes to high spirits.

The doctor hands out his advice candidly. He told one patient who has lost the fingers on his right hand, "Well, José, it looks like you will have to learn how to get along with the left. But be careful of that one; it's all you've got." José looked up, grinning self-consciously at the other patients, who were all staring at him.

The patients carefully discuss each diagnosis after the doctor has made his calls. For them, the Albergue, as cruel as it sounds, represents a learning experience, one of the few occasions in their lives when they will come into contact with educated people of the caliber of the Albergue staff.

On the third floor a women's ward holds thirty patients. Nearby, the laundry is done, by scrubbing sheets and clothes on boards. The patients are encouraged to take part. There is always some laundry to do.

Not long ago Sister Dulce had a small addition built onto the Albergue. Her pretext for getting the money was that the sisters in her order needed a place to live, accessible to the Albergue. But before they had a chance to move in, she turned the wing into a tuberculosis ward. The upper floor holds twenty women, the lower thirty men. Both floors are always filled to overflowing.

This is a source of friction between Sister Dulce and the doctors. They argue that she should encourage more of the TB patients to comply with the necessary paperwork to be admitted to the Santa Terezinha Anti-Tuberculosis Foundation. The Foundation, located in another section of Bahia, is a huge facility which is hopelessly inefficient. It is beset with financial and bureaucratic problems. In 1964 the Foundation had two thousands beds and only 250 patients. After paying off 250 staff members at salaries which have spiraled in recent years, the Foundation doesn't have enough money left over to feed more patients.

Several of the other health facilities in Bahia are plagued with similar problems, mostly traceable to bureaucracy. A doctor remembers sending two patients in mid-March to another hospital which should have been in a position to care for them. They went accompanied by letters from the doctor. They were told to come back again on April 1, and then again on April 14th. And still they were not treated. "This procrastination with everything, X-rays and so on, is terrible," according to the doctor. "As a result patients take to treating themselves. TB patients often dose themselves with drugs they've heard about and build up an immunity to them. For that one reason alone, some eighty to eighty-five per cent of the TB patients in the Albergue won't be leaving."

Distrusting the care of the poor at other hospitals, Sister Dulce puts little or no limitations on the capacity of the Albergue. She is reluctant to let her patients get lost in the shuffle at inefficient hospitals. But the doctors argue that she must. And another doctor added, "She must stop the infernal practice of admitting tuberculosis patients into the Albergue at night, when a doctor is not around, and letting them sleep in wards where they might well infect other patients."

Sister Dulce does not, of course, consciously attempt to frustrate the doctors, for whom she has a childlike reverence. But her consuming desire to serve knows no bounds. The Albergue, under her guidance, is as big as the day's needs. When there is a sudden surge of patients, additional beds blossom out of every nook and cranny. On some occasions the corridors of the Albergue have been completely filled with the sick. The Refuge across the street can, when needed, provide a place for hundreds more. In its first twelve months of operation the Albergue and the Refuge saw to the needs of an estimated 35,000 people. One senses in the Albergue a capacity for compassion, a heart which is as big as the day's demands.

7

Volunteers

Over the years many Brazilian doctors have helped Sister Dulce. They are, if anything, more giving of their professional services than doctors in the United States, according to an American doctor who served with them in the Albergue.

Typical of the Brazilian doctors is Dr. José Stanchi Corrêa, a graying man in his late forties. He comes to the Albergue whenever he can sandwich in the time between the two other jobs he holds. During the morning he works at the Santa Terezinha Hospital, where he, like other doctors, chafes under the frustration of administrative delays and misman-agement. In the afternoon he works for the Division for Tuberculosis of the state government's health agency.

At the Albergue Dr. Stanchi devotes himself to patients in the TB ward. Asked why he volunteered his service to the Albergue, he casually loosened the strings on his face mask and said, "Oh, Sister Dulce has more X-ray film than anyone in Bahia. At Santa Terezinha, you practically have to fight for film. But here it's different. Plenty of film. I told Sister Dulce as long as she keeps me supplied with film, I'll come gladly. Besides, I like it here."

Dr. Stanchi is one of several Brazilian doctors who comes regularly to make his services available free of charge to Sister Dulce's patients. The problem is that the help offered by many Brazilian doctors has to be irregular, so that it doesn't interfere with their own professional commitments in private practice. According to Sister Dulce, frequently Brazilian doctors begin working with her enthusiastically, but as their own practices grow, they have less and less time for her patients.

Nonetheless, Bahia's doctors have been extremely generous. Sister Dulce can't remember an occasion when she was not able to prevail upon one of her doctor friends in an emergency. But it has been a constant worry, especially since occasionally she worries in anticipation of her needs.

That's why she was so extremely grateful for the full-time service rendered by three American doctors who volunteered to help her. Each of the three doctors had his own reasons for going to Bahia to help Sister Dulce.

The first was Dr. Frank Raila, a handsome graduate of Loyola University of Chicago. Dr. Raila had a good practice in Chicago, but he also had some domestic problems which eventually ended in a divorce. He was sorely in need of a change, somewhere where he could get a fresh perspective on life and his own problems. This is important to mention in connection with Raila because frequently those who set out to help Sister Dulce are looking for something which she seems able to help them find.

Dr. Raila offered his services as a doctor free of charge to the Brazilian government, thus giving up a thousand-dollar-a-week practice in Chicago. At the suggestion of a friend in the U.S. Embassy in Rio de Janeiro, Raila was put in touch with Sister Dulce. Shortly before Christmas 1961, Raila arrived in the Albergue.

Within a short time he lost himself completely in his work. He lived next door to the Albergue in a room on the third floor of the Workers' Club of Bahia. With his easygoing manner and soft voice, Raila worked wonders in converting the Albergue into a real hospital.

Up until his arrival the Albergue, true to its name, had been a sanitarium, a comfortable haven in which to rest, and a clearing house for patients on their way to other hospitals. What was needed before Raila's arrival was an administrator in the Albergue, a person capable of gently prodding Sister Dulce into regularizing its business.

As matters stood, Sister Dulce was the source of everything; from her pocket came the money to buy essentials and to pay the "wages" of full-time helpers like Big Edna and Iracy. Wages for the Albergue's permanent staff fluctuated according to what Sister Dulce could reach with her right hand.

Dr. Raila filled the need for a hospital administrator for two years. He set aside regular hours for medical clinics in the Albergue. He developed a staff out of volunteer and poorly paid helpers. He raised the standards of all Albergue activities. And he did all of these things so quietly and unassumingly that no one, not even Sister Dulce, whose confidence he earned, objected. During his stay in Bahia, all elements, including the other sisters in Sister Dulce's order, were welded into an effective hospital team.

Sister Superior Alberta helped by allowing Sister Dulce wide discretionary powers in interpreting the rules of the order. Born in Münster, Sister Alberta has a rather characteristic Teutonic outlook on matters relating to discipline. Modifying her attitude was no mean accomplishment. The gulf that separates her from Brazilians, even after a quarter-of-a-century's service in Brazil, is enormous. Recalling a postwar vacation in Germany, she said, "Oh, what a delight it was to see Münster again! You know, it is really much prettier now than it was before the war."

While Dr. Raila was in Bahia, Sister Anacleta, a venerable

and faithful worker, assumed responsibility for the children's wards. Sister Marta oversaw the TB wards, and Sister Roma brightened the women's ward with her presence and devoted attention. One additional sister, Sister Umelina, helped out whenever she had time left over from her own heavy teaching schedule at a nearby school.

Dr. Raila's example of tireless dedication was an inspiration not only within the Albergue, but also within the city of Bahia. Shortly after his arrival, local American businessmen in Bahia organized regular and invaluable support for Sister Dulce's work through the American Society of Bahia. Within the Society the leading advocate of Sister Dulce's work was an American businessman, Bill Brokaw, the son of a Protestant minister. Brokaw had been in the automobile and auto-parts business in Bahia for fifteen years. One day he came unexpectedly upon a woman dying in the street in front of one of his stores. He spent the better part of the day telephoning hospitals to see if he could get the obviously destitute woman admitted. But without luck. Then, as he later said, "A hospital I phoned mentioned Sister Dulce, and I called her. In about twenty minutes here came this tiny nun on foot, almost running. Together we lifted the nearly unconscious young woman into a pickup truck which Sister Dulce commandeered on the street and we took her to Sister Dulce's chicken-coop shelter." When Brokaw saw what Sister Dulce was doing for the sick and helpless, he continued, "I was ashamed of how little I had done for the community I had been living in for nearly fifteen years."

When Dr. Raila arrived, he and Brokaw joined forces to organize combined medical and milk distribution outposts in the heart of the alagados. Each outpost was the hovel of a woman who offered to give out reconstituted milk, obtained through Caritas and the Food for Peace program. The woman of the house boiled water in a huge caldron and poured in a box of milk powder. Then she added M.P.F. (a multipurpose food) and sugar.

Typical of the women was Maria Leal de Souza, a short and motherly woman, who wore her hair in a neat ponytail. Her own children stood by the door, passing out tips on when the milk would be ready to the children who began lining up in front of her house at six in the morning. Thin arms held out tin cans for the one large dipperful each child under twelve received. In all, fifteen hundred children in Bahia's alagados received milk every day for nearly two years through this modest program.

Before Dr. Raila had been at the Albergue many months, he began writing to charitable organizations in the United States and to medical colleagues to beg supplies for Sister Dulce's work. In several instances he was extremely successful. For example, World Medical Relief, Inc., an organization established by a Detroit housewife, Mrs. Irene Auberlin, sent bundles of supplies. In ten years of existence, the WMR, which started at the initiative of one woman who wanted to do something, has distributed many millions of dollars' worth of medical supplies around the world. WMR solicits supplies from physicians, hospitals, and drug manufacturers. The supplies are expertly packaged by volunteers under the watchful eyes of trained volunteer chemists and registered druggists. Then they are sent through various channels to clinics and hospitals around the world.

Raila's hard work marked the beginning of an increased flow of materials from the United States. Up until the time he helped provide Sister Dulce with supporters in the States, the Albergue had been almost entirely dependent on Bahian contributions. This is not to say that Raila solved all the problems; that would have been an impossible feat. But he tried to establish some channels of communication for the flow of supplies to Sister Dulce's work.

By perseverance he was able to make sure that Sister Dulce received what she needed in the way of Food for Peace allotments. He tried, not entirely successfully, to establish in the minds of American friends and the U.S. government that Sister Dulce's organization did not serve only Catholics but poor people generally. Backing from the American Society of Bahia, largely a Protestant organization, was a help. So were American friends who realized that poverty in Bahia is no respecter of religious affiliation. Brokaw spoke for many when he said, "So she's a Catholic and I'm a Protestant, so what! Kids suffering from malnutrition don't know the difference."

Together Brokaw and Raila had to tread a narrow line when it came to Sister Dulce's own outlook. "Obviously, she is dominated by a 'Help now and pray later' attitude," said Brokaw, "but it's difficult to sell this idea to Americans, Catholic and Protestant alike, for different reasons."

Whatever was left over and above Sister Dulce's own needs at the Albergue was sorted by Sister Dulce's brother Aluisio and Dr. Raila and distributed to other charitable organizations in the Bahia area. But it was, and still is, difficult to convince skeptics that Sister Dulce operates in a frame of reference oriented toward the needs of the poor rather than toward the teachings of the Church.

The presence of an American doctor was a tremendous plus factor, though. As Sister Dulce herself says, "An American doctor seems to be the only way I can reach people in the United States with my message." Raila's presence was of equal value in stimulating interest among cultivated Bahians in Sister Dulce's work. Maria Angela de Carvalho, for example, the daughter of the rich baron who keeps Sister Dulce's gold book, was, she said, "Like other young ladies, much attracted by the handsome American doctor. He made us feel a little ashamed of ourselves." When she met him at a social function, she asked how she might help.

Raila replied, "Why don't you help us by writing some letters for Sister Dulce?" An accomplished linguist, Maria Angela reads and writes English extremely well. But like other young ladies of the Bahian aristocracy, she had not had much chance to put her talents to work. It is still a novelty to encounter a well-bred Brazilian lady working.

The Carvalho mansion, ruled by her stern father, was Maria Angela's prison. Built in 1950, according to the plans of an American architect, the mansion is sumptuous and impressive. They say that all the Italian marble that went into it, and the freshly cut long-stem flowers which today grace classical urns in the larger rooms, were made possible by wartime U.S. foreign aid.

U.S. technicians were sent to demonstrate on Carvalho's lands how rubber trees could be planted in between the rows of cocoa trees. The purpose of the program was to increase the hemisphere's rubber production during the war, when the Japanese conquest of the Far East had cut off supplies of this strategic material. The net result of the program, as far as Carvalho was concerned, was the accumulation of tremendous wealth through the revitalization of his extensive plantation holdings.

For a short time Maria Angela had broken away from home to do volunteer work in a school for the blind—long enough to learn how to read Braille as a "seeing person." But apart from a chance to escape from home, the work provided her little satisfaction. The school was hopelessly inefficient and poorly supported. The tragedy of the blind in Brazil, and elsewhere in South America, begins at birth. Brazilians frequently hide blind members of the family deep in the bowels of the home. They do not like to acknowledge blindness, perhaps, as a doctor suggested, because of some primitive belief that blindness betrays a taint in the blood or perhaps just because they are so sensitive about it.

Later Maria Angela was permitted by her father to work with her brother, the younger Joaquim, in her father's office. One day in the office, with the four-feet-square oil paintings of senior partners, the family crests, and the oak decor all looking down on her, Maria chanced to hear of the young American doctor from a friend. She learned he would soon be single. "That's why I went out of my way to meet him at a social function," she said candidly.

Since then, Maria Angela has been a capable and efficient collaborator, answering all of Sister Dulce's English language mail. She has devised form letters to handle sudden floods of mail, occasioned by several magazine articles dealing with Sister Dulce's work. Each letter has the stock phrase, "I am having this letter written by someone else." But each letter is freshly typed, not because it would be impossible to use a duplicator, but because Brazilians are accustomed to throw form letters into a wastebasket without so much as a peek inside. Indeed, any self-respecting Brazilian has a secretary who is instructed to throw form letters away for him. It is only by personalizing each letter that Sister Dulce gets her message across.

On the advice of her banker friend, Sister Dulce asked Maria Angela to request American donations in the form of checks drawn on U.S. banks so that Sister Dulce can take advantage of fluctuations in the exchange rates. By holding checks, sometimes she can get more mileage out of them. On occasion the amount of fluctuation in exchange rates from day to day staggers the imagination. Shortly before the 1964 revolution, at the height of inflation, it was reported that a housewife in Rio de Janeiro did her shopping at the supermarket early in the morning to avoid the afternoon price rises.

For a brief period Maria Angela tried to keep up with the bookkeeping. But being a woman, even with Brokaw's support she couldn't exert much pressure on Sister Dulce to provide her with the information she needed. Sister Dulce has never been known to take the advice of a woman very seriously in regard to business decisions.

It was to Sister Dulce's chagrin that Brokaw and Raila ganged up and insisted that she try to arrive at some estimate of the financial needs of her network of charities. With characteristic suspiciousness of systems and organizations, Sister Dulce, nonetheless, allowed them to bank the money she begged. Brokaw worked tirelessly to figure out the bills she had outstanding and to pay them off. As a curb on Sister Dulce's instant generosity to everyone, Brokaw signed the checks. As repugnant as the check-signing was to Sister Dulce's Brazilian way of doing things, she went along with the irksome process because of her admiration and respect for the two Americans. She acknowledges a great debt of gratitude to them both.

Raila and Brokaw put Sister Dulce in touch with many charitable organizations in the United States, from which she was able to solicit badly needed supplies. Philanthropic organizations in the United States have been extremely generous in their support of Sister Dulce. Among those most active on her behalf, in addition to the World Medical Relief, Inc. of Detroit, are Catholic Relief Services, the Meals for Millions program in Los Angeles, and friends in the city of Los Angeles itself.

In recognition of his efforts to coordinate the flow of charitable materials to organizations in Bahia, Bahia's City Council authorized Bill Brokaw to speak for the city when he traveled to the United States in 1963. Brokaw tried, with only modest success, to enlist U.S. government support for Bahia's own "Alliance for Progress," repeatedly making the point that foreign aid could best be handled through responsible local agencies.

Unfortunately, U.S. officials could be only lukewarm about handling foreign-aid money through what looked on paper like a program dominated by Sister Dulce, and therefore, in their opinion, by the Catholic Church. The Food for Peace program, under the energetic and imaginative leadership of director Richard Reuter, was an exception. He realized that through existing organizations, some of them Catholic, the distribution of food could be handled more efficiently than through the cumbersome operations of Brazilian local government, which seems to become progressively less efficient as one works from the higher to the lower levels.

But Brokaw's dreams of a credit union and low-cost housing project to replace little by little the alagados came to nothing. And the time that Brokaw poured unstintingly into furthering the cause of the poor in Bahia bore little fruit. He himself was subjected to criticism on the grounds that he was too visionary.

At the root of the criticism was the problem raised whenever there is the prospect that foreign-aid money will be made available to Catholic Church programs, no matter how unrelated they are to religious purposes. In Brazil, as in other areas of Latin America, where the Church claims two hundred million adherents, most people are Catholic. In the Brazilian Northeast, the Church is the only effective organization on the local, grassroots level. There are simply no other organizations of any kind or description, including government, which reach as many people as the Church.

To accomplish the social objectives of the Alliance for Progress, it is thus a question of working through existing and proven Church programs or creating whole new agencies at a tremendous cost in money and people. The Northwest Development Agency, with headquarters in Recife, is an example of the latter. SUDENE has been singularly unsuccessful in spite of the joint Brazilian-U.S. commitment of nearly half a billion dollars to SUDENE's success.

The difference between Sister Dulce and SUDENE is trust. Sister Dulce derives her strength from the people, to whom she has become a revered figure. SUDENE has developed into a political football; its chief architect and administrator was exiled from Brazil because of his Marxist leanings in 1964.

In only a few instances have U.S. officials taken an enlightened attitude toward working with the Church, and one must remember that the officials in turn must justify every penny spent to Congress and the American people. In Peru, U.S. loan funds were made available to support an admirable credit union movement run by the Maryknoll Fathers. As a practical matter many U.S. Peace Corpsmen, including Protestants, have found it expedient to work closely with local priests, who are often the driving force in isolated rural communities.

But the perplexities of the problem of working through the Church remain unsolved. As Sister Dulce herself says, "The Church has been behind the times in Latin America for so long that I can see how it's difficult for people to understand supporting Church programs." Indeed, up until recent years, a standoffish attitude toward involvement with the Church might have been justified in Latin America. But there is so much evidence now, since the famous pronouncements of Pope John XXIII, of a Church awakening to the primacy of social development that it is difficult to see how foreign aid in the social field can possibly avoid collaboration with the Church at some points.

Within Brazil enlightened new bishops appointed to five key areas of the Northeast issued *An Emergency Plan* aimed at doing something about social problems of that vast area. In Bahia the spirit heralded by the *Plan* is typified by the youthful Bishop Walfrido Viera. Bishop Viera believes, as does Sister Dulce, that people who are unable to clothe and feed themselves adequately are unable to partake spiritually of the Church's teachings. His view is a long way from that held by the Spanish and Portuguese conquerors of the New World, who felt impelled to baptize the Indians at any cost for their own good. In essence Bishop Viera advocates a wider Church role in raising the standard of living of the masses before undertaking the spiritual tasks, such as bringing them into closer communion with the teachings of the Church.

Bishop Viera is proud of the fact that the first marriage he performed in Bahia was between a widower and an ex-prostitute, each of them with children. The prostitute had been rehabilitated through a program run by a Jesuit father.

Elsewhere in the Brazilian Northeast, Catholic priests are organizing labor unions in much the same way that Sister Dulce organized the Workers' Club back in the thirties. Padre Antônio de Melo Costa, whose parish is in the town of Cabo, near Recife, is one of several Catholic priests who are trying to organize labor unions, to guide the Northeast's social revolution along non-Communist lines.

Father Melo's voice grows husky with emotion when he talks of the woes of the peasants. At such moments he calls to mind Padre Hidalgo, the priest who sparked the Mexican Revolution more than a century ago. Father Melo himself was reared as one of fifteen children on a plot of land too small to support his family.

Father Melo sees the future hope of the Northeast to lie in increased industrialization of the big cities. "Industries are needed all the more because of the migration of peasants to the cities." The Roman Catholic Church, according to him, is the only force in the communities of the Northeast which reaches down to the level of the common man. He feels that the Church must play a major, indeed indispensable, role in organizing people to realize social progress. He himself runs a school for bright young men on how to organize unions. "There is no such thing as a bad government," he said, "if men can express their dissatisfaction through organizations."

This revolution in Church attitudes is a fairly recent occurrence. When Sister Dulce began, she was in a sense a real precursor of what is happening now within the Church. The difference is that now she is not alone. One of her friends, Father Eugênio Veiga, Rector of the Catholic University of Bahia, is typical of a new impetus within the Church.

Father Veiga rushes around Bahia in a pea-green Volkswagen sedan that his students recognize at a glance. He beep-beeps at them spiritedly. Beneath the level of this joviality, Veiga is a stern believer in discipline. While he makes it a point to mingle with students and to get to know their problems, he doesn't believe that good relations with students should stand in the way of academic discipline. He is proud of the fact that his was one of extremely few universities, perhaps the one university, to stay open every day during the 1964 Brazilian revolution. This is amazing in the light of the record of other Latin American universities, where student strikes or stay-at-homes over relatively trivial matters are extremely common.

Father Veiga talks at a feverish pace, brightening his conversation with humorous anecdotes. When he was in the United States for the first time, he remembers learning three things: "How to wash my socks in a hotel sink; how to carry fifty pounds of luggage three hundred yards in a hurry; and how to have three whiskies before dinner, three during, and three after, and still be in condition to thank my hostess for a lovely evening."

Veiga is a crusader when it comes to believing that students should be familiar with the development problems

of their country. Recently he took several students on a trip
to see the new hydroelectric power station at Paulo Afonso,
an outstanding contribution to the development of the region.
He told them, "Those Texans [the U.S. technical advisors]
said we couldn't build such a big dam without more steel.
Steel is scarce in Brazil. We built it anyway, with very little
steel. That's your job—to find ways to build things without
steel, to find Brazilian answers to Brazilian problems."
Perhaps that kind of attitude helps explain why Veiga admires Sister Dulce. In spite of her lack of organizational
method, she gets things done.

Frank Raila understood this facet of Brazilian pride.
Quite apart from his excellence as a medical doctor, he
contributed enormously to the organization of the Albergue
by quiet and subtle determination, preferring to make do
within the frustrations caused by the lack of system to in-
troducing unrealistic changes for the sake of efficiency. When
he left, there was a little ceremony at the Albergue. People
cried. His photograph was hung over the doorway to the
emergency room where he had spent so many days and
nights. On the wall beneath it there is a simple but powerful
message, "Gratitude of the Albergue St. Anthony, 8-2-63."

While Raila was working in the Albergue, he was joined
for a few months by a second American doctor, Dr. Joseph
Bachman. According to Bachman, he went to Bahia to live
and practice medicine—temporarily at least—in a tropical
backward country. A youthful doctor and a bachelor, he felt
that it would be wise to get this desire out of his system
before settling down to the responsibilities of a private practice. In a sense Bachman wanted to test himself in a situation
where he would find himself overwhelmed by the number of
patients and put to the test of making do with relatively
simple facilities.

He was attracted by Sister Dulce's charm and earnestness;

as he said later, "I wanted to know this person better." Like other American doctors, Bachman was slightly disillusioned to discover that clinical medicine was one of the least urgent needs of the alagados. "My patients were miserable: materially destitute, illiterate, superstition-bound, completely cut off from the spiritual and material advancements of Western Civilization. Their greatest needs were basic education, training in hygiene, adjustment to an urban way of life."

A specialist in internal medicine, Bachman discovered that patients treated on one day turned up as patients on another. "Starving infants could be treated for kwashiorkor, but many of them would return in a few months in the same condition because of the poor diet and contaminated water supply." Bachman stayed for four months, from July to November 1963, when he was drafted for active service with the U.S. Army Medical Corps.

He especially admired Sister Dulce because, in his words, she was guided "by the virtue of charity, rather than the 'modern' concepts of social service and community development. Although she was organizing and supporting many projects to help the poor, she was realistic about successes and failures. She realized that it was impossible to do everything for this community, but that it was important to do something. Her hospital had limited facilities, but it was clean. The care available was not always the most modern, but it was given warmly and in a Christian manner."

Before he left Bachman came to respect Sister Dulce's medical skill, too. "Sister was fairly adequate as a diagnostician. I learned to take her medical opinion seriously. She knew without X-rays which patients probably had tuberculosis, which ones were psychosomatic. After all, she had run the hospital without the aid of an M.D. for several years."

Bachman recalled with amusement the way Sister Dulce seemed to understand men. She kept him well supplied with cigars that she begged from a local cigar factory. "Somehow she learned," continued Bachman, "of the North American taste for the dry Martini, and presented me with a bottle of gin on my birthday."

Bachman's stay overlapped with that of the third American doctor, who had agreed to take Raila's place for a year. The new man, Dr. Jack Curns, left his practice in Waukegan, Illinois, in the hands of his partner. Curns, a Purple Heart veteran of service as an infantryman in the Pacific during World War II, arrived in Bahia with his wife and two small children.

Curns wanted to do something. Enjoying the material comforts of a successful practice, he and his wife, Eileen, were much interested by what they heard about the Papal Volunteers for Latin America, a Church overseas service organization, modeled in certain respects on the U.S. Peace Corps. Curns volunteered to pay his own way for one year overseas. Since he was a doctor, the Papal Volunteers decided to forego in his case the usual frills of training, which includes intensive language-training. Looking back on his early months in Bahia, Curns sardonically recalled, "I spent more time studying medicine than I did Portuguese."

Tropical diseases that had been studied only cursorily in medical school, where doctors were preparing themselves for practice in the temperate zone, absorbed his immediate interest in Bahia. He had, he acknowledged, heard about tropical diseases in medical school, but he had forgotten them in his practice. One of the diseases is Chagas disease, an afflication that is frequently fatal. Chagas is caused by the bite of the reduvid bug, called *barbeiro* in Portuguese, which emerges from the walls of poorly constructed hovels at night and infects people with a disease which is incurable. A person so bitten develops symptoms like those of heart disease, a lot of swelling and enlargement of the heart, and commonly dies within a year or so.

Much more commonly, Dr. Curns encountered schisto- somiasis, or "snail disease." Snails drop tiny organisms in the water. When people go wading or swimming they pick up this disease through worms or blood flukes that lodge them- selves in the liver.

Two of the most common diseases he found to be worms and tuberculosis. Estimates vary, but tuberculosis is ex- tremely common in the alagados. Approximately 25 per cent of the patients in the Albergue have tuberculosis. Curns found all kinds of worms extremely common, too: round worms, hook worms, pin worms, "and even plain old garden variety worms."

Malnutrition is almost universal in the alagados, according to Curns. As he explains it, the children are generally breast- fed. During their first nine months or so, they seem to be bright-eyed, happy—probably at the expense of their mothers. But soon a new child crowds them out.

At about a year, mothers begin feeding their children a diet with extremely little substance. It is almost exclusively compounded of *farinha,* a starchy food made by grinding up the roots of the manioc plant and mixing this dust with water. The result is a bland, pleasant tasting substance with little nutritional value. According to Curns, "Farinha is roughly equivalent to methyl cellulose, which we use back in the States for reducing diets." Within a short time, children fed farinha contract worms or kwashiorkor, a severe protein de- ficiency. Sometimes at the stage when children develop a premature greying or reddish tinge to the hair, the illness can be corrected by a good diet. "But many of them," said Curns, "are brought to the Albergue too late and they die. A few children died in my waiting room simply because their mothers were too polite, or too ignorant, to realize the serious-ness of the disease."

Leg ulcers are also common, especially among men. Al-though he tried hard, Curns was unable to heal these ulcers with skin grafts. He thinks he failed because leg ulcers are very slow to heal.

The list of diseases Curns and the other doctors routinely treated could be extended indefinitely. Diseases like whoop-ing cough, measles, mumps—all of them left unattended within the hovels of the ignorant people of the alagados—while relatively easy to treat, ate deeply into the time that Curns had left over to study leprosy and smallpox, diseases that were far more stubborn.

While her husband was boning up on medicine, Eileen Curns was touring the alagados, she said, "just to see if I could cheer up people." She went with Sister Dulce the first time; and Sister Dulce recommended against Eileen's taking her own children along. But the next time Eileen did take along her five-year-old Jimmie, because she wanted him to understand his father's work. She remembers Jimmie's first reaction to the spectacle of intense poverty, when he saw children his own age. "Look, Mommy, they don't have any clothes on." After that Jimmie became a regular visitor to the non-communicable disease wards in the Albergue, to cheer up people on his own.

Eileen turned journalist while in Bahia, writing several excellent columns for the hometown newspaper, the Wau-kegan *News-Sun*. In one of them she described her reactions to Carnival in Bahia, a festive celebration that precedes Lent. She said that she and her husband began to realize the significance of Carnival when in November a patient who needed a minor operation said he would come back for it after Carnival. Her husband, she said, "frequently had a hard time getting patients to leave the Albergue, but before Carnival it was easy."

Although Carnival itself spans the last three days before Ash Wednesday, it is preceded by a couple of weeks of warm-up parties. The mayor of Bahia, in a major bid for popular support, had the main street of Bahia hung with colored lights at public expense so that people could dance in the streets at night.

The people flooded out into the streets to dance in costumes that had been sewed with care in preparation for the annual event. Someone reported seeing a nun, about Sister Dulce's size, in a costume and mask which completely concealed her identity, dancing too.

"The people," as Eileen noted in her column, "danced at arms length, not so close as in the States." Their costumes were bizarre, mostly the devil and his helpers. "The people laughed easily, where we might not think something was funny. If they didn't laugh so easily they might be depressed."

Eileen and Jack danced, too, as long as they were able. Then, like some of the less stout-hearted Bahians, they went home for a brief rest. Some of the people take a nap right on the street before beginning to whirl once again. To excite themselves, Bahians spray the air with an ethyl-chloride spray from a small shake-up can. Worn out by physical exertion, the people sleep between bouts of dancing as if drugged.

But the important thing about Carnival, Eileen noted, was that the poor people from the alagados feel a mystical power while they are hidden behind the masks of Carnival kings. "Carnival is the great blowing off of steam," she says. "After Carnival it's hard for agitators to work up much enthusiasm for anything. Some feel that Carnival is the salvation of the poor. During Carnival they use up enough energy for months."

Eileen was at her husband's side for his first major surgery at the Albergue. The operating room was given by a rich Jewish family which had come into contact with Sister Dulce much as the American businessman Brokaw had. Members of the family found a sick Negro child in the street. Attempts at getting him into a hospital failed so they brought the child to Sister Dulce. The family was so impressed by the remarkable way in which she accepted the child without hesitation that they decided to help her by buying all the equipment needed for an operating room.

Two photographers and a reporter from a local newspaper were on hand for the first major surgery. The photographers had their cameras cocked ready to get a shot of Dr. Curns scrubbing up for the operation. But the foot-operated soap dispenser didn't work. So he and a Brazilian colleague lathered up with a bar of soap. After scrubbing up, the doctors put their hands in rubber gloves, but the gloves had dried out in the tropical heat. Several pairs gave way, exposing bare fingers.

When the operation finally got underway, the water in the operating room stopped flowing because a plumber was doing some repair work in the nearby shower room. To complicate matters further, the patient had been given a spinal anesthetic, so he was aware of all the commotion around him. To relieve him, Eileen tried to pull loose a piece of hose that had been wrapped around his arm to slow down his circulation. But she wasn't strong enough to pull it loose because the patient's arm had swollen considerably during the confusion.

Her husband helped her out by cutting it loose. Then, undeterred by these delays, he went ahead with the operation. A big fly flew in through the window and buzzed back and forth over the incision. Finally the fly settled down on

Eileen's arm, complicating her duties as the circulation nurse.

These annoyances heightened the interest with which the Albergue's staff and some patients watched the operation from a window, quietly cheering the doctor on with whispered prayers and vows to the gods of the Candomblé.

"It felt like my first operation anywhere," said Curns. "Operations at St. Therese or Victory hospitals in Waukegan were simple by comparison." The patient survived. Within a couple of hours he was asking for something to eat; the next morning he was sitting up in bed, feeling fine.

Mention of the service rendered by Americans would not be complete without adding the name of Dennis Gates. In between his sophomore and junior years as a medical student at Loyola's Strich School of Medicine, Gates read an article about Sister Dulce in the *Saturday Evening Post.* He wanted to help, but, as he said, "Finances were a big problem ... I didn't have very much money in the bank."

So Gates demonstrated that Brazilians are not alone in having *jeito.* He wrote letters to twelve pharmaceutical houses, to see if they would be interested in helping him realize his ambition to work with Sister Dulce. One of them offered Gates a round-trip ticket by air. Gates worked as the Albergue's factotum for two and one-half months. In his off hours he made himself popular with the children by devising toys out of simple materials.

About a year and a half ago, the Albergue recruited its first registered nurse, an American, Lucille Lebeau, a native of New Bedford, Massachusetts, where her family still lives. Lucille went through the regular training of the Papal Volunteers. As part of her training, she spent four months at Petrópolis, Brazil, with a group of volunteers scheduled for scattered assignments in Brazil. Petrópolis is a beautiful highland resort town, not far from Rio de Janeiro and was once the summer residence of the last of the Brazilian emperors, Dom Pedro Segundo. There she received intensive language-training and indoctrination in Brazilian culture.

Lucille had agreed to serve four years in Brazil. She now occupies the green room, as she calls it, on the third floor of the Workers' Union, previously occupied by Dr. Raila. As the chief staff person of full-time duty status, she has inherited the position filled by Raila, Bachman, and Curns, minus the duties in the operating room.

A slim girl in her twenties, Lucille's willingness to live in the section of the alagados is a tribute to her remarkable courage. At first, she admits, she was a little frightened by being the only American girl; she was slightly ill at ease walking at night down the street from the Albergue to her room in the Workers' Union. But soon she became known as Sister Dulce's devoted helper and the luster of the Sister rubbed off on her.

Lucille is on call twenty-four hours a day. Sometimes she worries that the Brazilians won't waken her in the middle of the night because they are too polite or else because they fail to realize how serious an emergency is. She remembers one night when a Brazilian doctor was answering night calls in the Albergue. Lucille was the only one with the key to the pharmacy and the Brazilian doctor needed a particular medicine. But the Brazilian hospital assistant refused to go and wake her. The next morning Lucille tried to placate the Brazilian doctor, who was understandably furious over the incident, but characteristically Lucille couldn't get mad at the girl who had refused to wake her up.

Lucille relies heavily on Edna for advice on how to handle sticky situations. Lucille remembers one day when Edna turned to her and said, "This patient isn't telling the truth." Lucille replied, "How do you know?" Edna replied, "I know my people—they're so damn poor that they frequently have to forego the truth to get some medicine or a glass of milk."

Lucille works hard, in fact all the time. The only break in her routine comes when occasional friends within the group of Papal Volunteers stop overnight with her in the extra bed in her room. Her room is attractive, well furnished by previous occupants. Her refrigerator, a great luxury, is always filled to overflowing with fruits and the soda pop which Sister Dulce lavishes on her.

Once she complained without thinking of some bites she had received during the night. Later she was sorry she mentioned them because she found that a brand new mosquito net had been hung over her bed.

Lucille is supported by funds provided by her diocese. Since she comes from a rather poor diocese, she feels guilty about spending anything on herself. Mostly, she spends her modest income on the Albergue, a few toys for the children, and so on.

One of the things that has impressed itself on Lucille, as it has on other Americans, is the resignation to death on the part of the poor. She remembers a recent case involving a thirty-year-old woman who was in the final stages of terminal cancer, suffering a great deal from dysentery and vomiting.

In their ignorance the other patients in her ward told the dying woman to shut up so they could get some sleep. Lucille asked one of the young girls in the ward to help her change the bed. But the girl said that she didn't see why anyone should help a woman who was making such a fuss. So Lucille started to remake the bed herself. "It wasn't until the day after the woman died," said Lucille, "that I recalled how much she had suffered."

When Lucille visited the ward a couple of days later, she asked as cheerfully as she could: "Where is Maria?" Then she saw that Maria's bed was now being occupied by another patient. And she added, "Did she go up to heaven?"

"Oh, no," replied one of the other patients in the ward, "she died."

According to Lucille, this response is typical. "The poor seem to look on death differently from us. We don't like to mention death. They don't mind at all."

Like several other women who help Sister Dulce, Lucille feels that Sister Dulce is a man's woman in the sense of being bold, independent, aggressive, and so on. Sister Dulce prefers to deal with men, perhaps because of the structure of traditional Northeast Brazilian society, which in general has no place for women who work. A well-brought-up young woman puts it another way. She feels that women tend to be put off because of Sister Dulce's use of feminine guile. "Sister Dulce," she says, "is not at all afraid to weep profusely to gain her objective."

Lucille's duties do not end with nursing. She has become a trusted adviser to the patients and staff of the Albergue. As a Christian, she has the right to baptize children, pouring water over the forehead and repeating the traditional phrase, "I baptize thee, so and so, in the name of the Father, the Son, and the Holy Ghost."

In addition to the volunteer Americans and the Brazilian doctors, Sister Dulce has many other unpaid helpers. Indeed, the little knot of people who gather around her wherever she stops is comprised of people who can be instantly pressed into service.

She is like a military field commander, ready to improvise on a moment's notice to beat her enemies. Interruptions, changes in plans never cease. She takes advantage of each new opportunity, copes with each new crisis.

One day a little barefoot boy came to a running stop in front of her, smiled broadly and announced, "Someone has given the Albergue a dentist's chair." "Oh, that's very nice," replied Sister Dulce, "will you please go and get a dentist to come and have a look at it. Before the dentist arrives, be sure that the old man, whose teeth are bothering him, is in the chair."

Sister Dulce enjoys recruiting the people around her for special roles. She is like a Hollywood director in setting up certain scenes. Once, after she had heard that some particularly important officials were going to pay her a call to learn about the Albergue, she went to the Refuge to select someone for a bit part. She wanted to impress the visitors with the realities of her problems. So she asked a particularly emaciated beggar to explain to the visitors his story, speaking clearly and distinctly. She asked him not to change his ragged clothes, which, of course, he wanted to do right away when she told him about the visitors. She coached him to show to the visitors his lean arms, all the while explaining the circumstances which brought him to Bahia in the first place. This sounds rigged and it is. But Sister Dulce knows all too well that if she doesn't lay a little groundwork, no one will talk to the visitors about the unpleasant aspects of life.

The poor are afraid. No matter how poor they are and embarrassed, like human beings at all levels of society they want to show visitors the best. The trouble is that they are so inarticulate; few can express rudimentary abstract ideas. An adult must be coached to answer the simplest question.

"These people," said Sister Dulce, "live in conditions that are subhuman, worse than animals." If Sister Dulce occasionally directs them, it is because she must in order to get her story across. There is a warmth of understanding and love between Sister Dulce and the poor that takes the place of words. She seems to sense their needs. She has to because frequently they don't have the remotest idea of what their needs are, apart from immediate drives like hunger and fatigue.

Fortunately, she has been lucky in attracting to her work

a few Bahians with the power to reason. Adalicio de Almeida Santos, for example, is an extremely intelligent and sensitive young man. His large brown eyes dominate a thin, sharply chiseled face, giving him the look of a Frenchman. Adalicio was a well paid bookkeeper in a local bank before he suffered a nervous breakdown. The public health doctor gave him a note admitting him to a local hospital.

But even after undergoing rest and care for several months, Adalicio could only return to work part time at the bank. The bank told him to wait until he felt completely well again. Adalicio chafed under enforced idleness. Away from the regularity of work, Adalicio felt at a loss for something to do. "And I felt confused," he said, "disoriented. I had lost my religious faith, and I had a great many other problems—stemming from reading too much Sartre and Heidigger, I guess."

He heard about Sister Dulce. So rather than remain idle, Adalicio became a volunteer worker, offering to do anything she needed done. Sister Dulce installed him in a combination office and bedroom, the former admitting room for patients in the tuberculosis wing. Adalicio set about bringing the books up to date, starting from the excellent job Bill Brokaw, the American businessman, had done before his business forced his move to Rio de Janeiro.

Within a short time Adalicio had brought everything up to date. With the precision of a watchmaker, he now arrives at her debits and credits by dividing up the donations of material goods and money into several categories. Each month, sometimes more often, he presents her with the master copy of her financial statement.

Sister Dulce takes it into her lovely hands, as she stands hovering over Adalicio's desk. Adalicio leans back in his swivel chair, rests his arms, the sleeves of his finely made shirts—his only apparent extravagance—rolled up.

Sister Dulce's eyes light up at the sight of the neatly lined-up columns of figures. She says, "Hmm, let me see." In between exclamations like, "How will we ever pay this!" or "Is there no end to the money we spend on electricity!" Sister Dulce slides a finger down the list of expenses. When she has finished, feigning that she has it all in mind, she turns to Adalicio and thanks him profusely for his thoroughness: "Adalicio, where would we be without you?"

Adalicio smiles modestly, with penetrating humility, knowing full well that she couldn't care less than she does about the intricacies of her finances. What she has grasped from the maze of figures is the total: how much money she will need in all. From then on, each day or so she will pop her head into Adalicio's office and ask, "Adalicio, how much do we need today?"

Or she will return in the evening to pile on his desk a roll of money, her bankroll from the day's begging; some assorted cans of food; and other odd bits and scraps she has collected that day. More likely than not, she will find Adalicio bent over the typewriter. Like Maria Angela he never duplicates even form letters. A yearly letter, two full single-spaced pages reporting on the status of Sister Dulce's enterprises and requesting continuing support, is typed out individually by Adalicio for each of more than one hundred local business firms.

Adalicio now pays all the bills, banks the money Sister Dulce collects on her begging rounds, and tries to plan ahead financially, surprising Sister Dulce occasionally with sums of money she thought she had long since spent. In addition to this load, Adalicio keeps himself available twenty-four hours a day, since he sleeps in his office off the tuberculosis ward.

According to the Brazilian system of workmen's compensation, Adalicio continues to draw his salary from the bank. It amounts to nearly $270 a month, a sum he gives to the

Albergue to buy extra but not indispensable things, like furniture, radios, and so on. He feels it's a bargain. "My work at the Albergue keeps my mind off my problems." He wants to go on working at the Albergue over an indefinite period. His efficiency and total dedication have been of inestimable value to Sister Dulce. She considers him her most valuable Brazilian helper.

There are always so many jobs to be done in the Albergue that anyone who wants to help is welcome. Domingos Passos, a pharmacist who works not far from the Albergue, drops in whenever he feels like it to mix ointments for leg ulcers. A volunteer, he, like the others, asks nothing except to be of service.

Sister Dulce tries hard to be loyal to her helpers. She remembers them in tiny ways that are meaningful, such as sending a card or commemorating a birthday. But she realizes that nothing she can do will ever compensate for helpers enough. And she seems to feel that their real compensation should be derived from their labor among the poor, quite apart from any material rewards.

One does not sense any particular idealism as a motivation for helping Sister Dulce. Nor is there any standard of service rigidly imposed, like fixed hours or fixed ways of doing things. Each day there is a renewal of an offering of charity as fresh as a new flower. As for the future, one can only speculate that if Sister Dulce were to be gone tomorrow, so would be the helpers who are drawn to her today by Christian love.

8

Raising Money

A FEW years ago Sister Dulce revived her childhood interest in acting to play the starring role in a twenty-minute documentary dealing with what she is trying to do for juvenile delinquents in Bahia. The film was shot on location by a talented Bahian photographer, Leão Rozemberg.

As the film opens, the camera dollies in on a young boy, rolling over in his bed, the threshold of a doorway, his feet sticking out over the sidewalk. The boy rubs his eyes, yawns with hunger as the sun's rays open the curtain on a new day.

The boy scratches himself, moves out onto the street to look for something to eat. In the open-air market, he spots a fruit vendor. The boy sidles up to the vendor's stall to snitch a piece of fruit, a luscious orange, while the vendor with studied nonchalance looks the other way.

As the camera moves in close once again, the screen is filled with the cheeks of a policeman, puffed out like balloons around a shiny whistle. The whistle pierces the quiet morning scene, not once but several times. The boy flees, leading the policeman a tortuous chase.

Down the narrow street the boy runs, the policeman in hot pursuit, and then through an alley festooned with laundry. As the boy climbs a fence, the policeman closes the gap. With his height, the policeman has an easier time than the boy in scaling the fence. But like a Keystone cop, once over the fence the policeman blunders on past the boy who has taken refuge—behind the ample skirts of Sister Dulce, which are billowing out in a gentle breeze.

Once the coast is clear, the boy emerges and looks around. He pulls out a soggy-looking cigarette butt from beneath his tattered rags. He gropes for a match. At that moment, Sister Dulce, who has been nothing more than an immobile, expressionless hiding place for the boy, makes her first move. It is beautiful.

She reaches into her flowing robes and she produces a match. The camera catches her outstretched hand head on, holding a burning match to light the undernourished boy's smoke.

Using the rehabilitation of this boy as a narrative thread, the movie unwinds. Sister Dulce puts the boy to work, bundling up old newspapers which she sells to make money for the Albergue. At first the boy loafs on the job, ferreting comics out of the stacks of newspapers. But eventually the milk of Sister Dulce's human kindness make an impression even on this hardened delinquent. He develops a sense of guilt. He becomes a useful junior citizen.

Sister Dulce is a superb actress. On camera for more than half of the film, she is never at a loss as to what to do with her hands. She walks well before the camera, handling her robes with dexterity. In all, it's a lively film, marred only by a corny sound track, readings from the Bible, which were dubbed in after the film was made.

The fact that a nun should star in a film about her own work illustrates the lengths to which Sister Dulce has been driven to sustain her good works. The Albergue was scarcely a year old when Brazil entered into a period of deepening financial crisis that Sister Dulce had to weather if the Albergue was to survive.

The crisis began in August 1961, when Brazil's new president, Jânio Quadros, who had been inaugurated a few months earlier, resigned unceremoniously. Quadros had been swept into office by the biggest plurality of any Brazilian president. His campaign, symbolized by the waving of a broom, raised popular hope that he could do for Brazil what he had done for the State of São Paulo, where he had made a crackerjack record as governor. During his governorship, São Paulo had become the industrial giant of South America, the city with the lowest unemployment figure of any city in the Western hemisphere. Brazilians with reason referred to São Paulo as the nation's locomotive, the other states as the boxcars.

Quadros' quixotic departure from the Presidency threw Brazil into turmoil. His successor, João Goulart, proved incompetent from the start, when the Brazilian Congress, at the insistence of the military, stripped him of most of his powers to save the country from utter anarchy. Amid uncertainty inflation nearly overwhelmed Brazil. The year 1963 was an indicator of the price Brazil paid for its dangerous experiment with political inaction. The cost of living rose by 80 to 90 per cent. Changes in cabinets to appease popular demands for action provided fuel for Brazil's economic deterioration.

In Bahia Governor Magalhães said, "The federal government is my worst enemy. I can't even make up a yearly budget for this state because the inflation is so bad." Brokaw, the American businessman, said, "It is reaching the point where I don't dare sell anything anymore. By the time I buy a replacement for the things I have sold, my profit will have been completely wiped out. I can't mark up the price of merchandise fast enough to make a profit."

To support the Albergue Sister Dulce was forced to become an opportunist. A *Saturday Evening Post* editor, writing a story on the troubled situation in the Brazilian Northeast, with its stirrings of peasant unrest, arrived in Bahia at eight-thirty one evening. By ten he had an invitation to tour the alagados with Dr. Raila and Brokaw and to have lunch with Sister Dulce to hear firsthand the problems she was having in caring for the sick and destitute.

Teodoro Moscoso, at that time the U.S. Coordinator for the Alliance for Progress, attended a banquet in Bahia and found himself sitting next to Sister Dulce. After dinner Sister Dulce showed him, David Rockefeller, the president of Chase Manhattan Bank, and U.S. Ambassador Lincoln Gordon, the scrapbook she sat on during dinner, filled with pictures of her work, testimonials from the press, and so on.

The pressure of her growing obligations challenged Sister Dulce's ingenuity in dreaming up new ways of raising money. Occasionally she would, in moments of dire need, stuff bills into envelopes and send them to her friends. Important officials, like Governor Magalhães, received birthday cakes made in the kitchen at the Albergue. Beautifully decorated, the cakes were the platform for the figure of a small boy holding out a real blank check in his confectionery hand.

It was this method of raising funds that gave Dr. Curns an idea for helping her obtain a new, sorely needed vehicle. Through a golf-playing friend back in Waukegan, Curns invested six thousand dollars in candy. Local friends sold the candy everywhere, on street corners, at civic and sporting events, and so on. "They even sold a box of candy to the girls who work in the Fanny Mae Candy Store in Waukegan," said Curns. The profit amounted to about three thousand dollars, enough to buy Sister Dulce the Chevrolet pick-up truck she uses in her work.

Sister Dulce's fame was spread by the Brazilian press. A national magazine called her the "Angel of the Slums," an epithet that found a ready response from Brazilians, who were becoming aware of the immense problems of growing city slums.

In October 1962, Sister Dulce was invited to the United States to speak before the National Conference of Catholic Women in Detroit. Since she speaks a limited amount of English, she needed an interpreter and as usual, as she said, "God helped." Her interpreter, Mrs. Florence Goodrich, the widow of an American Foreign Power Company executive who had spent many years in Bahia, found the way of helping Sister Dulce that she had been looking for.

Mrs. Goodrich, like Governor Magalhães and others, couldn't shake from her mind the remembrance of her first visit to see Sister Dulce at work in the alagados. "I felt I couldn't go on living without doing something for Sister Dulce and her work. I couldn't sleep nights after seeing with my own eyes the immense misery and suffering of the children she was taking care of. So little by little I became an active supporter of her work. And the Sister knows how to take advantage of willing hands."

Mrs. Goodrich enjoyed accompanying Sister Dulce around the United States. At one of their first stops, Washington, D.C., they were sitting together over lunch in a restaurant, discussing Sister Dulce's problems with an American friend. The waitress overheard snatches of the conversation on the way to and from the kitchen. Just as Sister Dulce and her friends were about to leave, the waitress slipped a white envelope into her hand, saying, "I find that whenever I do anything like this, the rewards are a thousand-fold." The Sister accepted with a strange reluctance this casual donation. That night when she opened the envelope she found a crisp twenty-dollar bill, the waitress' entire day's wages.

In Washington she was invited to meet the press in the offices of the Food for Peace program adjacent to the White House. She handled herself like an old pro, making news in all three Washington papers. Later on the same day she was invited to share honors with a well-known Brazilian movie actress at a reception in the Brazilian embassy.

During the day, apparently the story of her good works was gossiped around the embassy. The highlight of the evening was the Ambassador's presentation of a check for funds raised during the working day from among members of the embassy staff.

When she was introduced to the Director of the Agency for International Development, the U.S. foreign aid agency, she was not at all timid about espousing the cause of the poor. She listened patiently to the director's words of greeting. He said, "The news of your wonderful work has touched my heart." She could stand it no longer. "I didn't come all the way here to touch your heart," she said, "I came to touch your wallet." Whereupon she produced a detailed list of her needs which Adalicio had drawn up: an eggbeater, four more lanterns, twelve bed pans, and so on—carefully itemized—in all worth about five thousand dollars.

But the director could do nothing. As he explained, politely but pointedly, his job permitted him to be interested only in bigger things, loans and grants worth millions of dollars. Sister Dulce was undeterred; she left his office, as she had the offices of countless Bahian businessmen who had been forced to turn her down, without a trace of bitterness. And she was comforted by her gratitude for the help and assistance she had already received from the United States. "Whenever things are darkest," she said, "I look to America for help."

When in Washington she went one morning to see the White House by joining a regular public tour. Like many Latin Americans she felt a deep warmth in her heart for the late President Kennedy. She would have given anything to meet the President, but it was impossible and she accepted this denial gracefully. When later they received the news of his assassination in Bahia, people openly wept. They gave flowers and fruit to American officials in his name. A woman wrote to a friend in Washington to ask, "The next time you see Jacqueline Kennedy, be sure and express the sympathy of the people of Bahia."

One of the highlights of her trip to the United States was a visit to Los Angeles. There the promotional efforts of two energetic advertising women, Ellie (Mrs. Monty) Walker and Marge Crawford had paid off handsomely for Sister Dulce's cause. The two women worked long and hard to promote a sister-city affiliation between Bahia and the city of Los Angeles as part of the Sister City Program of the American Municipal Association. Through this affiliation, which was signed by officials of both cities in September 1962, the two cities have a continuing exchange of people and cultural understanding. For its part, Los Angeles has shipped enormous quantities of medical supplies, building materials, and clothing to benefit charitable organizations of several denominations and to further the work of public charitable organizations as well. The tie was particularly appropriate since it was from Bahia that California obtained the cuttings with which to start its navel-orange industry.

While Sister Dulce was in Los Angeles she appeared on the Art Linkletter television show, an appearance which stimulated many vitally needed contributions. A special dinner in her honor drew several Hollywood stars; Pat O'Brien was the emcee and Barbara Stanwyck read a script about Sister Dulce's life which had half the audience in tears, not to mention the actress herself.

Sister Dulce was slightly ill at ease to be the center of so much attention. She knuckled under to the demands of public relations only because it seemed to offer the prospect of raising the money the poor desperately need. In this instance, one might say that the end seemed to justify the means.

But the problem is that it is so difficult to get across the complexities of Sister Dulce's struggle and the needs of the alagados which she serves. Her ability to persevere in her merciful work defies simple explanation. Eulogies to her work seem to embarrass her, because in so many instances they are based on beliefs to which she does not subscribe.

The one difference she feels between those who eulogize her and herself is that she, Sister Dulce, lives day in and day out in the alagados. She feels she thus has an experience in understanding the poor of Bahia which few others possess. She is rather caustic about superficial examinations of the problems of Bahia's poor.

To her poverty is not something that can be eliminated. "There is no end to poverty," she says. Poverty, like wealth or beauty, is a manifestation of God's will. Thus she resents those who attempt to apply the success standard to the alagados. "The alagados are something you feel or you don't," she comments. She has no burning desire to change God's will as it is expressed in poverty, only to understand it.

This is a difficult message to get across. Sister Dulce's own growing legend obscures a fundamental truth: at no point in her day does Sister Dulce feel that she and her work are providing the way onward and upward for the people in the alagados. She and her helpers are merely comforting those in misery, and enjoying, if that is the right word, a closer relationship with God.

For North American ears Sister Dulce will occasionally cite this or that as a yardstick of progress. Over the past couple of years she has sent out figures on the number of patients treated at the Albergue. But these figures belie the more important point which the singer Caymmí gets across in his haunting voice: Life is an illusion. More than an illusion, life is to a very large extent foreordained.

It is this simple belief which enables Sister Dulce to be almost entirely free of any sort of recrimination against the poor or rich, because we are all playing roles assigned to us by geographical or paternal accident. As a philosophical ideal, this may sound very old-fashioned, and it probably is. But it has the virtue of a beautiful realism. Combined with a deep and abiding natural faith in God, it is the guiding force in Sister Dulce's life.

As in the case of Lawrence of Arabia, detachment from the forces and events which move ordinary mortals is part of the fascination of the legend of Sister Dulce. The poor are Sister Dulce's desert—just as sweeping, as majestic, as biting as the wind-whipped sand, just as gentle at rest, and as wholly engrossing on a pitch-black night.

There is a feeling in the still evening in the alagados, with here and there a kerosene lantern flickering, the comfortable nearness of the tropical sky and a bright moon dancing, of something at once attractive and evil. It is then that the light from the lanterns is diffused through all the cracks and crevices, creating a glow which unites the alagados to the glow of cities all around the world. One feels the universality of the poor, and identifies oneself in the warm light with the drives that move men everywhere.

There is really no way to publicize what moves Sister Dulce and these people. Such an unusual and intricate set of circumstances, so far removed from the normal daily experience, must be seen and felt to be understood. Chance or fate seems to play the most important role at every step of Sister Dulce's way.

A few months after Sister Dulce's life story, as read by a Hollywood actress, had melted the hearts of those who attended the dinner in Los Angeles, the mayor of Bahia arrived

there as the guest of the city. Whether moved by some un-
known pique or by plain old-fashioned cussedness, he made
a speech which was widely interpreted as being extremely
anti-American, thus undoing some of the good will which
Sister Dulce's visit had inspired.

Sister Dulce returned to Bahia, longing to put her hand at
the helm once again. In Bahia, she is vastly more at ease.
There she can raise money at the drop of a hat, where money
is to be had. Whenever the State of Bahia's contribution to
the Albergue is brought up in the Chamber of Deputies,
Sister Dulce takes along a couple of boys and stands in plain
view of the assembly behind a glass paneled door. The ex-
posure of herself and the boys to the deputies helps along
their deliberations.

In between the Chamber's formal sessions, she does a little
lobbying with the deputies she knows especially well. Occasionally the Chamber passes a special appropriation to help
her over a particularly bad period. In 1963 the State gave her
a million cruzeiros (about $570) in July and another million
and a half on Christmas eve.

During the April 1964 revolution in Brazil, Sister Dulce
kept herself as well informed as her friend, the commander
of the Sixth Army, who is in charge of the military in the
State. Fearing that civil strife over a prolonged period, with
the markets closed, might cause problems in feeding and
caring for her patients, she had to be abreast of the situation.

On Saturday, with the revolution to break out in the early
hours of Monday morning, Sister Dulce was busy stocking
up on supplies. She put in a call to the new governor of the
State to remind him that now might be as good a time as any
to make good on his promise to supply her with some fish
from the state-run refrigeration plant. The governor agreed.
He realized a little popular support might be needed to keep
himself in power.

Fortunately the revolution occurred without bloodshed, although there was a purge of all leftist elements, which to some observers looked like the beginning of a witch-hunt. The wife of the mayor who had made the inappropriate remarks in Los Angeles called to ask Sister Dulce to intervene on her husband's behalf with the Sixth Army Commander. But there was no saving the mayor; he was shipped off into exile along with other leftists. He had, in spite of the good words Sister Dulce may or may not have said on his behalf, done little for the poor except string up the lights at Carnival time.

Nonetheless, she did affect a polite interest when she was informed that as the mayor was being shipped off into exile, his wife screamed up at the departing ship, "He's not a Communist. He's not a Communist."

"Oh, poor thing!" Sister Dulce exclaimed softly when she heard the news, without specifying whether she meant the mayor or his wife.

9

The Farm

ONE day Sister Dulce came upon a boy of about ten sitting forlornly in a dirty alley. She asked him, "What is your name?"

He replied, "Thing."

"Is Thing a name?" she asked.

"That's what I'm called," he replied, matter of factly.

"Do you have a mother and father?" she asked.

"No," he said, looking into the nun's eyes, "do you want to be my mother?"

Sister Dulce hugged the boy. She took him home to the Albergue with her, where he played with his first toys and where she gave him a name, Antônio.

Antônio is Sister Dulce's favorite name; there are hundreds of Antônios in Bahia who received their names under similar circumstances. Antônio to her is the child of neglect, symbolic of Bahia's homeless children. Within Bahia, young delinquents like Antônio, are known by the romantic name of "Captains of the Sand," because at night they sleep on the beaches by the sea. During the day they prowl the streets, picking up cigarette butts, stealing candy, or simply being idle.

The cause of rehabilitating homeless boys, whom she calls "her little thieves," has always been close to Sister Dulce's heart. For years she has ferreted them out of the streets or out of the jails. Three boys she had released from jail called themselves "Midnight Vampire," "Little Rat," and "Cheating Tongue." "If they ever had Christian names," Sister Dulce said, "they had long since forgotten them."

And for years Sister Dulce has been mentioning the plight of these boys to whoever would listen. Once she halted the presidential motorcade of the late President Getúlio Vargas, when it was passing through the streets of Bahia, with a human chain of boys, hands joined together. To the astonishment of the President, she spoke up for them in her usual soft voice, "When are you going to do something for my boys, Mr. President?" The President, a strong-willed chief executive, admired her derring-do. He promised to look into the matter.

Some years later, Governor Magalhães succeeded in urging the state legislature to pass a measure paving the way for the donation of a state-owned piece of land not far from Bahia, at Agua Comprida, to Sister Dulce. The land had originally been earmarked for an experimental farm. But this project never got off the ground. Some shelters were built, a few so-called farmers were put on the payroll, but funds ran out and the farm became a boondoggle, the land an embarrassment to the state.

In the administration of Governor Magalhães' successor, Governor Lomanto Júnior, the land was formally deeded over to Sister Dulce. The farm thus materialized out of the confluence of Sister Dulce's conviction and the right moment.

The farm is a pleasant spread of land, comprising a gently rolling bowl of hills and considerable flat acreage through which flows a stream. It has an agreeable climate, back from the coastal humidity but not far enough back to be completely surrounded with tropical jungle. On one side of the property there is a little waterfall, from which the farm takes its name. Beyond the rolling hills, there is a fresh-water lake where no one dares swim because of the danger of small alligators.

The land is largely open. It has been stripped of almost all vegetation except for a few fruit trees. The soil is heavy and black. The farm thus affords plenty of space and fertile land, an idyllic place to rehabilitate boys. As Sister Dulce said, "It was the answer to my dreams."

The word "rehabilitate" rolls so easily off the tongue that it is perhaps in order to describe what the boys are like to begin with. They are small in size. One would underestimate their ages by three or four years. Most of them appear to be stunted in growth, slightly hunchbacked because the growth of their frames outpaced the nourishment they were given. Some are lame or crippled; others scarred and potbellied.

They are the result of a vigorous process of natural selection. According to Dr. Frank Raila's estimate, nearly 80 per cent of the children in the alagados die before their first birthday. Besides their squat appearance, the boys are routinely dishonest. They are accustomed to stealing everything in sight, whether they need it or not. As one of Sister Dulce's American helpers confessed, "It's been hard for me to develop a Christian love for the poor because they are so repulsive." They steal the fruit off the trees, food from the kitchen, but gradually, as they come to like the farm, they become less dishonest.

They are brutal to one another. Affairs among them are habitually settled with fists or worse. Like slum kids the world over, their gang instincts are well developed. The objects of their brutality change as do their loyalties to this or that leader.

In the presence of grown-ups they are customarily dour and staring. They seem to stare at everything. While they are so occupied, devious signs and gestures carry subtle messages among them. But let a grown-up strike up a conversation with any boy, and he will follow the grown-up around like an obedient dog, unrelentingly dogging the adult's footsteps and watching to see where he can possibly perform some little service to ingratiate himself.

Those of the boys who have had any association with parents at all picked up a body of superstition and nonsense that is a real barrier to doing anything for them. Warned of the coming visit of a doctor to give them routine inoculations, many of the boys took to their heels. Wise in their ways, Dr. Curns had them all assembled in the schoolroom at the farm and the door secured before announcing to them his purpose. But even so, a few of them escaped the shots, some because of their premonition of his purpose; others by scampering out a window. One ducked the shot-giving by pleading that he had to go to the bathroom, from which he did not return.

Like their parents they are unbelievably resigned to their lot in life. As Dr. Curns learned, "People will frequently accept the consequences of the death you predict for them rather than undergo a disabling operation. . . . While they don't take the doctor's advice, at least they have the courage to face up to their choice. . . . Very early in my experience here in Bahia, I became deeply impressed by the difference in the attitude toward death. The poor of Bahia accept death as an eventuality which they are powerless to change. One might say they are graceful in the face of death." This resignation is written all over the faces of the boys; indeed, among them it seems to be almost a cult.

They are almost animals in their normal behavior, crueler to one another than most species of animals, and totally disrespectful of law and order. By the age of eight or nine some have become hardened criminals. But then, one must remember that many of the parents of those fortunate enough to have had parents died before the age of thirty.

Ever since the days when she broke the lock on the door

to establish her first clinic, Sister Dulce has been taking some of these boys in tow. One carried water to the patients under the arches leading up to the Church of Bomfim. It is the only employment he can remember. Sister Dulce commissioned some of the boys to sell used furniture that came her way. Others she put to work collecting and stacking up newspapers. One boy ignited a pile of the papers by dropping a lighted cigarette on it.

When she opened up the Refuge, Sister Dulce put some of the more promising boys to work in sheds where she accumulated tools to operate a small business for making crude farm implements, trowels and shovels, out of odd bits of iron, and sandals out of discarded tires. "The boys are clever with their hands," she discovered, "but they work lethargically."

"They didn't have any place to play," Sister Dulce said. "I had to find some way to get them out of the city." Indeed, one of the differences between the children of the alagados and those born under more favorable circumstances is that the children from the alagados seldom seem to play unless they are driven to it or unless an adult plays with them. The farm provided a setting where the boys could enjoy clean, fresh air and the out-of-doors, scarcely a half hour's drive from the Albergue on a good road. "Just removing them from the temptations of the city was a step in the right direction," she said. Initially, she set the boys to building and repairing quarters for dormitories. A few Bahian friends came along to supervise. But, like the Albergue, in the beginning the farm was a makeshift arrangement.

Sister Dulce invited friends to come out and spend an afternoon with the boys. The policeman who had blown the whistle in the movie that advertised her work came occasionally to teach the boys some songs while he played the guitar. Sister Dulce borrowed a movie projector from the local office of the United States Information Agency.

The boys watched any sort of film, no matter how dull, with the same intentness.

Then, through Dr. Frank Raila's efforts, she heard of an American farm family which had volunteered for service in Brazil through the Papal Volunteers. In August 1963, Eileen and Lyle Mallary arrived in Brazil with their two daughters to begin three years of service. For the Mallarys, service in Brazil was their first experience outside of the United States. In the States they had made their home near Cordova, Illinois. About the time that their farm was optioned to permit the construction of a new highway, they began thinking seriously about realizing a lifelong dream of serving overseas.

Five of their seven children were grown and settled. Their remaining two daughters, Martha, twenty, and Margaret, twelve, were enthusiastic about their parents' plans. Apparently the idea of working in some type of missionary activity had been in the back of Mrs. Mallary's mind for a number of years. She absorbed with relish all the accounts of missionary work which she could lay her hands on. And, as she said with a smile, "Lyle always seems to go along with what I say."

Like Lucille Lebeau, the volunteer American nurse, the Mallarys spent four months in Petrópolis learning about the language and Brazilian culture. While they were there feverish plans for their arrival in Bahia were rushed through to completion.

Shortly before their arrival the American Society of Bahia entrusted Roy Lee Worley, the Moore-McCormack Line's man in Bahia, with enough money to have plumbing run into the farmhouse. Worley is the senior American resident in Bahia; he has lived there for more than twenty years. From his apartment, which is kept at sub-Arctic temperatures by a powerful air conditioner, he keeps an eye on the sea. From the window of his bedroom, which is hung with frosty snow scenes, he can spot through his binoculars incoming ships as they round the bend, turning from the open sea and making for Bahia's port. Then, nonchalantly, he has a leisurely shave and a cup of coffee before ambling on down to the pier in time to meet the arriving ship.

In recent years Worley has begun to look quite old, the combined effects of arthritis and of shaving off the red, dagger-shaped beard which everyone in Bahia knew better than his name. He has known Sister Dulce longer than any other American. His friendship with Sister Dulce's father dates back to the time when Sister Dulce as a small girl used to hold his hand while he was in her father's dental chair. Recalling that memory of years ago, Worley laughed. "You know how this town is. I was afraid people were going to talk. She was a beautiful girl. In fact, she still is beautiful—when she's not mad, that is."

"Sister Dulce," he says, recalling the time just before the Mallarys' arrival, "was anxious to lay her hands on the money for the plumbing for the farm so she could spend it on some more worthwhile purpose. She said, 'Lee, you and I have been friends for years. I promise that I'll get the plumbing fixed myself. Just give me the money.'"

Worley was hard-pressed. As he has discovered from long experience, "It is well nigh impossible to refuse her." Then, wandering away from his story, Worley remembered, "I said to myself, even when she was a mere youngster, 'That girl knows her mind.'" Whenever anything of interest to her work occurs on the waterfront, Worley lets Sister Dulce know about it.

When he received the message that the first shipload of Food for Peace was to dock at Bahia rather than at Recife, "because those foreign-aid boobs discovered that there were no grain elevators at Recife," Sister Dulce was informed. The ship docked in the afternoon. Scenting a possible dock strike in the air the next day, Worley cut short a beer with a friend, saying out loud, "You know, there is nothing that says I can't unload that ship tonight." Brokaw and Raila, representing Sister Dulce's interests, were there on the wharf as huge hoses vacuum-cleaned the hold of the ship and piped the grain into Bahia's elevators. Worley was as determined as they were to see that Sister Dulce should receive what she needed for the poor.

But in the matter of the plumbing he stood his ground. "Sister Dulce, you know that you are my friend. I'd do anything for you. But the money for the plumbing has been entrusted to me for one specific purpose and no other. I won't give it to you until you produce the bills for the labor and materials involved in getting plumbing for the house at the farm."

When the Mallarys arrived, they were in for a memorable surprise. With Sister Dulce they drove out to the farm, to find the dirt road leading up past the gate lined with boys. "There was a band, too," recalled Lyle; "they couldn't play for sour apples, but it was a band."

The boys fell into formation behind the triumphal march of the Mallarys. Sister Dulce made an eloquent speech of welcome and presented them with the keys to their new home. The farmhouse was in perfect order; the plumbing worked. "There were roses on the pillow, a mosquito net over the bed," recalls Mrs. Mallary. "It looked like a bridal suite. There were cards of welcome. All kinds of food had been sent out."

The honeymoon ended as swiftly as it had begun. The Mallarys found little time to concentrate on planting crops. Their first problem was discipline, the management of two to three hundred boys. Before they could undertake this task, they had to get together a list of the boys.

According to Sister Dulce's pronouncement on the matter, there were to be no locks on the dormitories or, indeed, anywhere at the farm. "This made it difficult to make a list," said Lyle Mallary. "The boys kept taking off on French leave whenever they felt like it."

Little by little, as the Mallarys gained the confidence of the boys, the boys chose to remain on the farm. The Mallarys organized them by age groups: five to eleven, twelve to sixteen, and seventeen to nineteen.

The boys were extremely superstitious, noted Mrs. Mallary. One day she discovered a small boy sprawled out in an epileptic fit. The other boys warned her to stay away from him. But Mrs. Mallary waded in and cared for him as best she could.

She took the unfortunate boy under her wing. A doctor at the Albergue supplied her with *dilantin,* a medicine for epileptics. She gave the boy his meals in the kitchen of the farmhouse because the other boys wouldn't eat with him. They were afraid that he would pass on his illness via plates and silverware.

Mrs. Mallary couldn't seem to convince them that this was not the case. Indeed, the epileptic boy himself was resigned to being an outcast. "Do you really use this cup too?" he asked Mrs. Mallary, when he saw her drinking out of a cup he had used. "Of course," she replied. "I always use the nearest cup."

When Sister Dulce heard about the boy, she, like the other boys, thought that he ought to be sent away for the good of all. "He will, I'm afraid, never fit in with the other boys," she said to Mrs. Mallary. But Mrs. Mallary is sticking by her guns, caring for the boy as best she can.

It was hard for the Mallarys to get used to sharing their lives with so many boys. There were times when they felt like packing up and going home. The boys were forever beating one another; they acted like gangs of delinquents.

But gradually the Mallarys are making progress, though it isn't always evident to them. "It's funny," said Lyle, "but you can see I'm pretty old to be learning a new language, Portuguese. I think the boys are beginning to take pity on me because of my speech handicap. As screwy as it sounds, I think my poor Portuguese is one reason I'm beginning to feel like I'm getting across to the boys."

There have been differences of opinion between Sister Dulce and the Mallarys over how to run the farm. Some of the differences, petty in nature, still baffle the Mallarys. For example, Sister Dulce is against putting in a window to let some light into the kitchen. After he had asked her permission to bang a hole through the wall several times and had been refused, Lyle figured that maybe Sister Dulce's opposition was due to the fact that she wasn't interested.

Lyle took matters into his own hands and poked a hole through the wall. "A little hole," said Lyle, "but what a difference it made." When Lyle was away from the farm on an errand, Sister Dulce had the hole filled up. "I just don't know why," said Lyle, scratching his head.

Sister Dulce insisted that the boys be paid for their work, as are the peasants who work on the big plantations of the Brazilian Northeast. This caused needless friction, according to the Mallarys; boys who didn't get paid felt hurt; the bigger boys got paid more. Some of the bigger boys made the smaller boys do their work for them.

The Mallarys had another problem in trying to live up to the expectations of the boys. "Sister Dulce told them that once we arrived, everything would go swell," said Lyle, "but it didn't." There were many heartbreaks. Lyle Mallary experienced many frustrations in adapting his knowledge of farming to the climate of the tropics. The Mallarys brought with them from the States twenty pounds of seeds, mostly vegetables like tomatoes and carrots. Together with the boys they planted the seeds in flats. The vegetables grew well up until the time for transplanting. Then they encountered their first enemy: rainfall.

The farm is well within the humid coastal strip where rains are sudden and torrential. Once the plants were in the ground they were completely washed out, in spite of frantic efforts at trenching around them to draw the water off. But Lyle Mallary didn't give up.

He watched his neighbors. He saw how they built *leis,* shallow flat mounds of earth eight to ten inches high, and eight to ten feet square. Around the leis they dug a network of canals. The system worked for Mallary too. He acknowledges gratefully his debt to his neighbors' technology. "From what I have learned of Brazilian methods," he says, "they do a pretty good job of controlling water, except for that month of April when two or three inches of rain fall per day."

He has so many other things to do that it is nothing short of miraculous that Lyle Mallary gets around to farming at all. He and his wife and daughters must oversee the supply of food. Twice a week someone must drive out to the national petroleum refinery at Mataripe, a few hours away, to pick up food. There in the kitchen Sister Dulce has a devoted friend. He saves all the leftovers from the tables and gives them to her to feed the boys at the farm.

The Mallarys estimate that these leftovers take care of 90 per cent of the food needed for the farm. They keep them in a big refrigerator in their house. Young girls Sister Dulce has pressed into service prepare the meals for the boys. There are so many boys that they have to eat in shifts. Long high tables are set out with their food by boys who have drawn K.P. The standard fare is beans and rice, rounded out by produce and fruit grown on the farm in an orchard which Lyle is cultivating.

The Mallarys' daughters have numerous jobs of their own. Martha keeps bank accounts for the boys. She helps the doctor when he comes to give them shots. Margaret, too, keeps busy. She bandages cut feet, and patches up boys who have been beaten by bigger boys. The daughters are a tremendous leveling force; in their presence the boys actually act civilized.

Then there is the broom business and the shoe factory, which the girls help run. Sister Dulce set up these industries to give the boys something to do and as a way to make money. The shops are located behind the farm flagpole where the Brazilian national flag flies alongside of Sister Dulce's own farm flag. The brooms are made out of a locally grown fiber, which is cheap to buy. There are several different models, ranging in size from a small broom good for sweeping off desks to a big pusher broom, the kind dear to people who have to sweep out garages.

The broom business is going well. Sister Dulce manages to hear who needs brooms and then to offer her brooms at a slight saving. When a contract for brooms was being let at the military base, she managed to find out the lowest among the "sealed" bids and she bid a few cents less. Sometimes she makes money on the brooms; at others she has only the satisfaction of underbidding the competition. But she always drums up enough business to keep the boys busy.

It gives them the chance to learn simple skills. They learn how to turn a handle on the lathe and how to bind up the fiber with a piece of tin sheared out of a tin can. They learn in a semi-grown-up way how to manage a small business. Older boys oversee the work; younger ones work as apprentices.

The shoe business is housed in a series of small shops, much like those the boys moved out of when they transferred the sandal business from the Refuge to the farm. Even tiny boys have a chance to cut out the simple designs. Some of the bigger boys have learned to make stout boots. As in other Sister Dulce enterprises, improvisation is the keynote.

The boys like the farm. Quite rapidly they seem to pick up the lingo of farming. They talk among themselves like experienced men of the soil, drawing liberally on precepts passed on to them by Lyle Mallary. In effect the farm represents an acceptable change of status for them from "Captains of the Sand" to farmers.

Gradually the Mallarys are eliminating hazing as a means of discipline. The constant terror felt by the younger ones, who formerly lived in fear of the bullies among the older ones, is being replaced by hard work and incentives. One of the incentives is to live, as two of the boys do, on a hill in a thatched hut and care for a cow and a couple of calves. There are, as a result of competition for important positions in the broom and shoe businesses, fewer and fewer raw hands from beatings by paddles or sticks. And more and more Sister Dulce is accepting the Mallarys' judgment on matters related to the operation of the farm, such as the moment when specific boys should be encouraged to leave.

There is no formal graduation ceremony. Once the Mallarys or Sister Dulce have reached a decision, Sister Dulce takes the boy aside, and she tells him it's time for him to look out for himself. Frequently boys aren't happy about leaving, but they are resigned to their fate.

In the morning, with a full stomach and a few cruzeiros in his pocket, the boy will leave. It is a touching scene, watching a boy walk off in the distance towards the city, so ill equipped to seek his fortune.

Sister Dulce tries to find jobs for them, but she can't in the majority of instances. In part the difficulty the boys have in finding a job is physical. A local businessman says he would really like to hire some of the boys to work in his chicken-raising business, but "they are so small and frail that I'm just afraid they wouldn't be able to wrestle with hundred-pound bags of feed."

Sister Dulce does the best she can. If a particular boy experiences insurmountable difficulty in finding a job, he knows that she will always readmit him to the farm, while she exhausts all the possibilities at her command to locate a job for him. The lives of the boys she helps are woven inextricably with her own. She never lets them down.

10

Summing Up

Sᴉꜱᴛᴇʀ Dᴜʟᴄᴇ is ceaselessly on the move. She had scarcely finished her morning cup of thick Brazilian coffee one day before she was called out on the street in front of the Albergue to care for a sertanejo in threadbare rags who had jumped down off the bed of a pickup truck which gave him a lift from Juazeiro, a focal point for migrant traffic from the interior of the backlands to Bahia. Before pulling away from the curb the truck driver gave a blast on his horn which shattered the early morning silence and caused Sister Dulce's coffee cup to jump in her hand. When she reached the man, she found that his lips were so burnt by the sun and his throat so parched from the long ride that he could barely speak.

Later on that day she had to stop by one of the local offices of the state's cumbersome bureaucracy, where she twisted the arm of a friend for the free license plates she would need for her vehicles the next year. She pointed out to him, "You will remember, my friend, that the green truck was after all a gift from the state to me, so it would be reasonable to expect that the state would want to supply the license plates, too." Without waiting for this remark to work its intended charm, she went on breathlessly, "Then, there is the matter of the other vehicles we have, my son. It would be reasonable to assume that the state would also want to license them free." With the plates under her arm she left, pausing at the door to press her earlobe between her thumb and forefinger, to signify success to the boys who were waiting for her on the sidewalk.

Later on the same morning she ministered to the needs of a man with deep knife wounds which he received the night before during a skirmish at a local Afro-Bahian rite. She reached him, fortunately, before the local shamans, who tend to complicate rather than cure wounds with bizarre remedies compounded of chicken livers and other remedies sacred to pagan gods.

She couldn't resist the temptation to stop and see if there was anything that could be done for the poor unfortunates whose miserable shanties, built too near the base of the promontory, were obliterated by a landslide brought on by a heavy rain the night before. But they had been killed and their bodies removed; there was nothing stirring except a thin column of dirt which poured from one of the few remaining boards in the roof onto the floor, like sand in an hourglass.

Motion suits Sister Dulce. She walks endlessly about her business. The graceful swing of her gait is somewhat offset by the dark scuffed Oxfords she wears. The cumbersome shoes appear as heavy as wooden Dutch shoes in the tropics, where sandals are the fashion.

As she walks, it appears that she is earnestly looking for something which is always just a little ahead of her. She trains her gaze well ahead, in the manner of a man carrying a heavy suitcase and afraid of bumping into something unexpectedly.

The tangible objects of her unending search are money and resources to satisfy her personal devotion to the poor. "In a sense," says a Bahian businessman, "she is the universal beggar. When you give to her, you give to yourself—at least I always feel that way." In this role, Sister Dulce has become not only a local but a national legend. Brazilians from Rio de

Janeiro and São Paulo, the great cities to the south, feel guilty about the national neglect of the Northeasterners, in much the same way some Americans feel guilty about the treatment of Indians. A recent movie of the sertão, Graciliano Ramos' *Vidas Secas,* an impelling drama of a family forced to leave their land by a severe drought, began with an announcement that it was high time that Brazilians took an interest in the third of Brazil's total population that lives in the Northeast.

Sister Dulce has become identified as the living symbol of concern with the problems of the Northeast. While she is not at all reluctant to use her fame as a means of obtaining funds, she is little interested in such broad concepts as national needs. To her the cause of the poor and her role in eliciting contributions for her programs is personal in nature, revolving about the plight of the single individual for whom she happens to be caring at the moment.

As a beggar she seems capable of striking terror in the hearts of those from whom she begs. A lifelong friend says, "I feel as if I had been drawn into an uneven contest whenever my conscience is pitted against her small talk and her wheedling ways." On this level Sister Dulce enjoys herself enormously. She laughs with fiendish delight when she recalls parting a selfish person from the money in his wallet. She sighs when she remembers how she spent the sum in her cause before a new day dawned.

She expresses herself largely through her eyes and her hands. Sometimes her eyes seem to roll on at her objective like breakers against the shore; at other moments, her eyes are quite still, anxiously waiting for something to happen. Without warning violent squalls, welling up out of an immense hidden torment, flash across her eyes. Then, just as suddenly, her eyes become glazed over and pale, seemingly becalmed.

While the mood she expresses with her eyes changes rapidly, often incomprehensibly, her hands tend to be more constant. One feels that the senses of her hands are acute, like those of the blind. She transmits warmth with her hands. A hand on the shoulder of a sobbing boy will reassure him, and he will almost invariably stop wailing to listen with rapt attention to what she has to say.

When she is seated, her hands turn and twist in her lap like the hands of a woman knitting. At such moments, her hands convey the impression of total absorption.

By contrast, words frequently betray her real motivations. Like an inexperienced baseball player, she tends to swing erratically at thoughts. On one day, she says that so-and-so is among her worst enemies; on the next among her most devoted friends. She seldom expresses with words the subtle shades of meaning between hot and cold that she does with her hands and eyes. She is careless about words.

She is equally careless about printed words. Shown a two-page, closely typed press release prepared in anticipation of her visit to Washington, she said it was exactly right. Later, when she was questioned by reporters about points in the release, she had answers quite contradictory to those in the release. To Bill Brokaw belongs the credit for having schooled her in the details of her own biography, which he pried out of her over a lengthy period of time.

It is ironical that these facts of her life have appeared in publications of the right and the left, though Sister Dulce herself is decidedly on the right. She goes out of her way to tell the poor, "Americans are your friends," a flat statement which has great influence among Bahia's poor. "I often wonder," said an official of the U.S. Consulate in Bahia, "if Sister Dulce isn't the reason for the difference between Bahia and Recife. In Recife there are interminable Communist uprisings, such as peasants taking over large estates. But here in Bahia there is very little of that."

Sister Dulce inherits her politics from her father, who is an archenemy of anything even faintly resembling Communism. Both he and his daughter have applauded the Church's strong stand against Communism. But one will try in vain to elicit from Sister Dulce an elaboration of her political convictions. Once she has declared herself on the matter of ideology, she, like most Brazilians, jokes about the foibles of Brazil's clumsy bureaucracy.

In discussing almost any matter, Sister Dulce is dominated not so much by what she says as how she says it. The sound of her voice seems to modulate her mood. When she is wistful, her voice, quite apart from the words she uses, is much more wistful. When she is angry or provoked, she swallows her words, and she speaks so rapidly that her soft voice stings even though her words may be scarcely audible.

Like the city of Bahia, Sister Dulce is full of changing contradictions. She seems not so much interested in discussing life as in living it. The daring pursuit of funds seems to satisfy her love of human adventure. She is the activist par excellence. "Her trademark is motion," said a Bahian businessman. "She knows everybody and everybody's business," said a politician, "and she is not above enjoying gossip and a remark or two with a barb. She has the politician's instinct for good timing. I really envy her. If she wanted to be elected governor, she could be—and she knows it."

Sister Dulce seems to thrive on people. She needs them. It is a part of her enchantment, her spell, that she needs company, much as Rima, the ethereal heroine of W. H. Hudson's *Green Mansions*, needed the jungles to the north of Bahia where ". . . Nature produces her effects at random, and seems only to increase the beautiful illusion by that infinite variety of decoration in which she revels, binding tree to tree in a tangle of anaconda-like lianas, and dwindling down from these huge cables to airy webs and hair-like fibers that vibrate to the wind of the passing insect's wing."

The beautiful illusion of the green jungles on which Rima depended for her existence is very close to the beautiful illusion of Bahia on which Sister Dulce, and indeed all Bahians, seem to depend. Bahia is in a sense the acme of illusion. There are the illusions of past glories, the illusion of life to which the singer Caymmí returns repeatedly in his songs, the illusion of Carnival which fills a burning need, and, as Sister Dulce noted, the illusion that life will be better in Bahia, which draws thousands of migrants to the city.

In the world of Bahian illusion, Sister Dulce is a link with reality. She is a constant reminder to the rich that there are poor. "The rich have become calloused to the sight of poverty," she says. "It isn't that they don't want to help. Frequently they do. But they have become accustomed to seeing poor people out of the corner of their eye. When they see a fat woman begging alms on the sidewalk in front of them, they think to themselves, 'Now, why should I give anything to that woman? She looks as though she has plenty to eat.' What the rich don't realize is that appearances are deceptive. They don't know that the woman's husband has just left her or lost his job. So, naturally, whereas yesterday she had enough for herself and her family, today she doesn't. But I must admit, in fairness to the rich, that some people exploit their situation and try to live by begging when they could work."

Indeed, some of the poor fit themselves out especially for begging. The practice of borrowing babies to use as stage props in begging is not uncommon. Some beggars appear to have regular routes laid out which they follow each day. A particularly haggard old woman makes the rounds of hotel lobbies. "So what if I do?" she asks. "There are always new people staying in the hotels who haven't seen me before. And look at me, I'm some sight, you must admit!"

Brazilians tend to admire such good-natured cleverness. They admire it in Sister Dulce, although a few are put off by her use of feminine wiles. A women's group offered to help her by buying beds for the Albergue. To their chagrin, when the ladies picked up the bill at the store, they found that it covered only the first installment on the beds. Also on the bill were the first payments on other things, like cribs and basins and so on.

When they confronted Sister Dulce with this fact, she merely replied, "You said you wanted to help. I didn't expect you to make all the payments." The point is that Sister Dulce did not consciously want to rob them of the thrill of paying for whole beds. She assumes that any person or group, which wants to help, wants to help like herself, with total dedication.

Sister Dulce's insistence on dedication has soured her relationships with some of her helpers who have responsibilities apart from Sister Dulce's personal war on poverty. One woman, whose husband worked for Sister Dulce as a doctor, was obviously eager to point up her failings. "She ate a piece of cake at my house," the woman said, "and you know, nuns aren't supposed to eat outside of the convent." Sister Dulce would willingly admit to this peccadillo; she adores, like all Bahians, the wonderful ices, made with fruit, which are sold everywhere on the street. She is a study in concentration as she licks a coconut, mango, or pineapple cone. She has to lean forward to avoid spilling the drippings on her habit.

The woman went on to catalogue other failings which added up to what she felt was lack of propriety or lack of the proper humility. "It's apparent that you are eager to tell the worst about Sister Dulce," she was told. And then the woman candidly confessed the real cause of her irritation. "She takes over everything," she said, "including your husband, if you let her. Why, she thinks nothing of asking my husband to work his fingers to the bone day and night. She doesn't know where human endurance leaves off. She expects everybody to be like herself, completely, but completely, wrapped up in *her* poor."

"*Her* poor" was at the heart of objections to Sister Dulce voiced by a beautiful woman from Pernambuco, a state to the north of Bahia, where there are many people with piercing blue eyes descended from the Dutch. This woman warmed quickly to the task of raking Sister Dulce over the coals. "It makes you mad," she said, "the way she feels she has a monopoly on the poor. No one but her can do the right thing."

Former Governor Magalhães cited the same unreasonableness on Sister Dulce's part. "I used to tell her, again and again, 'My dear, you are obsessed with the poor. It's not good for you or your work. You must rid yourself of this obsession; it's unnatural.'" The American nun who accompanied Sister Dulce for several weeks on her trip to the United States summed up her impression of the Brazilian by saying, "She is a wonderful soul, completely dedicated to charity. But so single-minded. Like many single-minded people, I think she suffers from a lack of understanding. She's really so impractical sometimes."

Dedication and single-mindedness are Sister Dulce's armor against the enormous excess of poverty she finds in Bahia. Whenever she stands back a bit and takes in the size and urgent complexity of the intense human suffering all around her, she becomes sad, even depressed. When she is separated for even a few moments from people, and something to do, she becomes quite helpless. She seems noticeably thinner and frailer when she is alone, curiously out of character.

She knows that neither she nor any person can minister to the needs of all. It is the hurt from this stinging realization that goads her onto the streets again. In helping she seems to find a relief from sorrow that she would not find behind the walls of a convent. It is difficult to imagine her confined within one, unable to communicate directly with the poor who, like herself, are restless and seething.

When she is discouraged she seeks out the companionship of children to restore her strength. They sense in her a kindred spirit. They enjoy her rambling conversation, her jokes, and her openness, partly because she doesn't talk down to them or tease.

She has the habit of observing and evaluating adults on the basis of their behavior with children. She can tell by the smallest incident whether a particular adult is truly responsive to children. If they are not, they do not have the quality she most prizes in her adult helpers, *dedicação*—sensitivity, respect, consecration.

Perhaps it is her love of children which explains her attachment to a worn copy of *The Little Prince*, by Antoine de Saint-Exupéry, which she guards, as zealously as she guards anything, in her desk drawer. She admires Saint-Exupéry's writing because, she says, "He knows how to awaken a sympathetic understanding. His book makes a person think."

When his airplane was forced down on the deserts of North Africa, Saint-Exupéry found comfort in the companionship of an imaginary boy, a prince from a strange planet. Faced with the prospect of death, Saint-Exupéry found solace in his conversations with the prince. After a long chat, in which the prince discussed the affairs of his tiny planet, Saint-Exupéry wrote, "Now my sorrow is comforted a little. That is to say— not entirely. But I know that he did go back to his planet. . . . And at night I love to listen to the stars. It is like five hundred million little bells."

Besides the solace Sister Dulce receives from excursions into the fantasy of the world of children, she is nourished by her complete attachment to the present. What she remembers of her own childhood is a prologue to her life now. When she is reminded of how once she was a football fan, taking a passionate interest in the fortunes of the *Botafôgo* team, she seems surprised, so dimly does she remember any other passion but her passion for serving the poor.

Only under duress does she remember anything at all about the interests she had before she became a nun. It is as if by taking the nun's vows she drew an opaque curtain between herself and her life before. Her strange ability to discard the past as irrelevant to the present is more shocking as one moves closer and closer to the present. She rapidly forgets the details of what happened last year, last month, even yesterday. She is so intent on the present moment that she has a startling capacity for unencumbering herself of anything which is not of immediate utility.

She tends to forget people who were among her most devoted helpers just a few years ago. The names of Brokaw and Bachman, and others, have slipped into a kind of oblivion. They do not stir up in Sister Dulce any great spontaneous show of gratitude or admiration. Not that this is due to any intended slight. Reminded of the part they played in launching this or that activity, Sister Dulce will bubble forth with their praise. But she doesn't do so spontaneously.

In this respect she is like the people in the alagados whom she helps. In gratitude they say, "May God repay you." One senses in this attitude on Sister Dulce's part a certain identification with universal values or drives which precludes intimate human friendships. Her one close and enduring attachment, to her father, is an exception.

It is explainable only because her father has devoted himself to her so totally, and with such utter dedication. In a sense, the normal father-daughter relationship has been reversed. He believes, as he repeatedly says, "She is a saint."

That he worships her is not an exaggeration; he most emphatically does. He is her disciple. He preserves her letters and the record of her life as if they were relics.

One detects a certain bitterness in Sister Dulce's younger sister, who is still at home, as she listens to her father sing Sister Dulce's praises. So engrossed does the elder Lopes Pontes become when he is discussing his daughter that he has been known to run head on into the fat old mangabeira tree across from the Carvalho mansion, and to narrowly miss death from an automobile hurtling down a narrow street.

Sister Dulce discusses every important move with her father. He is her record-keeper; frequently he works on the ledgers at home after Adalicio has put them away for the day. Lopes Pontes encourages his daughter and gives her hope. He retells the story of the moment when Sister Dulce was near death, suffering from a fever in a deep sleep. He reminds her and his listeners of how she gave out instructions for a simple coffin, and how she recovered her full health and vigor to the surprise of her doctors and friends. And there is never an unkind word said about his attachment to his daughter. For over a lifetime he has himself expended all that he has earned on charitable works.

Her father's support is invaluable to Sister Dulce. It is he who has helped to smooth over frayed relations between Sister Dulce and other charitable organizations angered at the way in which Sister Dulce seems to get the lion's share of donations and credit. Owing to his constant help, Sister Dulce can afford to concentrate on the present needs of her work.

She both suffers and is sustained by her attachment to the present. She suffers because there is too little time for her to get to know people really well. The one boy, her first patient in the house into which she had broken illegally, is an exception. Mostly she must help one and move on to the next.

The next she heard of the small freckle-faced red-head who

peeled his clothes off in her office, he had been bitten severely in the face by a dog at the farm. She arranged by telephone to have him admitted to one of the best hospitals by pleading for him with all her heart. She would have given anything to visit him. He was a very special boy with a rare intelligence and good humor. But she would have to wait and tend to her duties. Were she to take time out to visit him, perhaps the other children would hear that she had a favorite. And this she wouldn't risk.

No more than she could risk at another time squandering a few moments to go back on the road to look for the boys who jumped off the speeding pickup truck in which she and Dr. Curns were ferrying them to the farm. As the truck slowed down for a bend in the road, two or three of the boys jumped ship, taking off each with a pair of boots, from a pile of used clothing she was taking to the farm. The boys would sell the boots and make enough money for a weekend blast in town. Perhaps later they would wind up at the Albergue or the Refuge once again. Once again Sister Dulce would take them to the farm. But Sister Dulce couldn't take the time to hunt for them back along the road. There was simply too much to do.

Sister Dulce saves her strength to care for those who are suffering now. She seems to have a very highly developed sense for discovering those who are in anguish, an uncanny ear for a child crying, and for knowing in which hovel an old person is suffering out a terminal illness. Her presence is a continuing source of hope to those who have neither the warm bosom of family nor hope of recovery from the afflictions of poverty.

That she has become a legend in her own time is perhaps partly attributable to the mystical reverence Northeast Brazilians often feel for wise or giving people. Sister Dulce is the object of pagan as well as Christian praise. Not infrequently, a patient will invoke a heathen deity as well as the Christian God before submitting to an operation in the Albergue.

The price she pays for filling so many diverse roles, for answering like an oracle so many foolish questions, and for serving so many needs, is lack of organization. She has not built her charities neatly one on top of the other. The haphazard way in which her charitable activities have grown is illustrated by the ill-fated chicken-raising project she initiated a few years ago.

It seemed like a good idea to raise chickens on the farm. So she procured a load of baby chicks. Without proper care and inoculation the chickens contracted a disease. When a veterinarian told her that the chickens would all have to be killed, she was stunned. But she quickly recovered her composure and forgot about the whole matter.

The way in which she has launched out into one activity after another had been a continuing source of friction between Sister Dulce and her order. While the details of this friction are obscured by the veil of secrecy which surrounds matters within the sisterhood, the main outlines are clear. Superiors in her order have been repeatedly sent to Brazil to advise her to stop trying to do too much.

But Sister Dulce has remained unfathomable to the superiors in her order. She is so different, so Brazilian. To a certain extent she is the benevolent leader, following a tradition of leadership deeply ingrained in the history of Latin America. She is sometimes authoritarian. She runs the farm and all her other activities by consulting herself and her own conscience.

Like the master of a coastal estate, she not only looks out for the hired hands, who up to recent times were bought and sold with the land, but she also rules every aspect of their lives. She is Law and Order, spiritual guide and confessor; she is everything to the boys at the farm. To the chagrin of more conventional Catholics like the Mallarys, Sister Dulce expresses only mild interest sometimes in the ritual practices of Christianity.

"She doesn't make much of an effort to explain the meaning of Easter or other Church holy days to the boys," said the Mallarys. "She just doesn't seem to care at all about their souls. She says she is concerned with other important matters. But what could be more important?" A Catholic visitor from the United States remarked caustically after a tour of the farm, "I saw plenty of shoes, but damn few Bibles."

"The problem with this farm," said Lyle Mallary, "is that it's Sister Dulce's baby. She won't let go. It takes a long time to make a breakthrough." Ever since the Mallarys first arrived Sister Dulce promised them to get them a driver for the truck, so that Lyle wouldn't have to make all the runs to pick up food. "Then every time we got a driver we liked she would take him back," said Lyle. "This happened four times. When she wanted to take back our last driver, we got kind of mad. He was very reliable. We had trained him. Then out of a clear blue sky she wanted him back. We objected, but she was determined to use him to drive one of the Albergue's vehicles. Off he went. But a couple of days later he showed up again, walking down the road with his gear in his hand. He said that Sister Dulce had told him that he should go on working for us here at the farm."

This petty grievance is typical of those cited in connection with other activities run by Sister Dulce. At times she seems to be working at cross purposes with those who want to help her the most. Another failing of Sister Dulce's, often cited by her most devoted helpers, is her disdain for the status of women. She clearly prefers to deal with men. When asked why she doesn't encourage the other sisters in her order to take over some of the fund raising, her reply was razor sharp: "They're no good at it."

Mrs. Mallary echoed the complaint of several women who have stuck out working for Sister Dulce. "She's a lot cooler to me than to Lyle. She doesn't seem to notice what I say." This is not to say, Mrs. Mallary hastened to add, that Sister Dulce is consciously slighting her. It is just that Sister Dulce, her upbringing and the whole tradition of the Brazilian Northeast, would point to the relative unimportance of women in what is essentially a man's world.

Sister Dulce has enormous strength, partly derived from the flock of people who follow her around. In a sense this strength is both her greatest virtue and her greatest flaw. As Dr. Raila expressed it, "Sister Dulce has the ability to reach men of stature with her message, being such as she is—her smallness or the sense of fragility that seems to envelop her, plus the feeling one has that one must keep this Ming vase from being used to dig into the hard earth of poverty. But she is a lot tougher than one imagines. If we lived as she does, we would end up in an early grave."

In rebuttal to those of her helpers and those in her order who would have her loosen her grip on her activities, Sister Dulce's answer is disarmingly candid: "If it's God's work, God will help." Needless to say her stubborn adherence to this belief doesn't satisfy the questions raised by her critics. She resolutely refuses to take advice on matters related to her work, or advice which might impinge on her own freedom of action. She has never been known to follow a schedule for long. One of the doctors who worked closely with her said, after careful deliberation, "No, I can't think of anything she does in a really organized manner."

Sister Dulce is completely vital to every activity in which she is engaged. What if she had to withdraw for reasons of disability? Her answer: "God would take care of things." She refuses to believe that anything can be insured against loss through better organization or human means of indemnification.

On this and other questions, she is like some modern-day Antigone. Like Antigone, Sister Dulce is defiant of the rules imposed by governments and other organizations when they seem to be in conflict with the dictates of her own conscience. At times, it appears that she is willfully careless of the rules of her order. She is totally committed to her way of doing things, which is, all criticisms to the contrary, effective beyond belief.

This single-mindedness is the source of criticism and admiration. As a priest, who is a dear friend of hers, says, "Sister Dulce isn't a nun in anything except dress. As for belonging to an organization which is supposedly hierarchical, that's really a laugh—the thought of her as a well-greased cog in a Church machine."

In the priest's view, the days of individualistic charitable enterprises like Sister Dulce's are coming to an end. "The operation has grown to such size and complexity, and it is still so Sister-Dulce oriented."

There seems to be much evidence to support what he says. Sister Dulce is no longer alone in her devotion to the poor. She is supported by Protestants, Jews, and indeed by members of various sects. There are other programs which are doing splendid works for the poor, like the Seventh Day Adventist missions which serve large areas of the state of Bahia.

Many additional sects and organizations are building strong programs in support of the same objectives as Sister Dulce's. The Southern Baptists maintain a self-help center in Recife to the North; Presbyterian missionaries have long distributed food and clothing throughout Brazil's Northeast; and the Church World Service, the Lutheran World Federation and the World Council of Churches have all shared in trying to meet some of the most pressing needs of the Northeast's hungry millions. Recently the U.S. Peace Corps added its strength to social programs for the improvement of conditions within the interior of the State of Bahia.

Although her work is by far the best known, Sister Dulce is by no means alone in working for Bahia's poor. Major Cosme de Farias, a man of venerable age and appearance, helps the poor by standing in front of a certain church and offering passers-by the benefit of his years of experience. His is in the nature of a one-man counseling service for the poor, whose problems he knows intimately. A short, stocky ex-lawyer, Dalva de Mattos, manages, as her personal contribution to the poor, a sizable orphanage. Then, of course, there are several public agencies which are slowly becoming more effective instruments of social welfare. Thus, today there are an increasing number of charitable organizations which in the near future might carry on more efficiently portions of the program Sister Dulce has so heroically initiated. "After all," said the same clerical friend mentioned above, "since Sister Dulce relies wholly on her own initiative, she is as an institution limited by the number of things she herself can do." And then he turned his face away. He could not go on.

The people who have suggested changes in the way Sister Dulce does this or that are legion. Indeed no one who observes for any length of time the good works she has devised to serve the poor comes away unscathed by the desire to change something, if only to lighten Sister Dulce's burden.

It is almost as if there were some secret bond between Sister Dulce and the poor, which is beyond human comprehension. The bond manifests itself in her belief that a good deed today cannot give way to a greater good tomorrow. She listens so intently to the heartbeat of human affairs that one is hard put to describe what it is she hears. The invisible wall of intense sensitivity is the barrier between her and the people around her.

She is to a certain extent the artist whose sole means of communication is visual. In ordinary terms her life is as difficult to understand and as subject to interpretation as a canvas of the teeming city of Bahia.

Were the world peopled with Sister Dulces, it would be hopelessly confused and lacking in order. There would be nothing but random movement, based not on instinct but on an intelligence which can not easily be defined.

It is dishearteningly sad to consider the future of the poor she now serves. Few of them will ever leave a distinguishable mark even on their most immediate surroundings. The doors to higher education and achievement cannot be opened by anything she does for them. Of the boys presently on the farm, only one has any tangible prospect for a career, and that is as an enlisted man in the Brazilian navy.

Sister Dulce's efforts notwithstanding, the poor of the alagados will go on filling the books which deal with the statistics of want with the sad truths of their existence. This doesn't diminish Sister Dulce's fervent pace. She is far too sensitive to the cry of a child to be swayed by the criteria of success. Like the migrant in a popular song who sings,

> "I'm going to Maracangalha,
> I'm going.
> If Analia doesn't want to go,
> I'll go alone.
> If Analia doesn't want to go,
> I'll go alone
> With my straw hat,
> I'll go alone."

Sister Dulce is resigned to the journey she is making. Since there is in her real world no foreseeable end to misery, she never acts as if there might be. Like the poor, she accepts reality and is hopeful of heaven. That she perseveres in her merciful work at all is due to circumstances that could only have arisen in Bahia.

Her good works have taken their toll. She is pitifully underweight. She suffers from a chronic cough. At times, she seems to be fatigued beyond human endurance. Yet, tomorrow she will wake early, as she has for more than thirty years. One may rest assured that at this moment, Sister Dulce is doing something for somebody who has no one else.